AMERICAN HERITAGE

February, 1976 · Volume XXVII, Number 2

American Heritage has been selected by the Library of Congress for reproduction on recordings called "Talking Books," distributed free by regional libraries in the United States to those unable to use conventional print because of a visual or physical handicap. For information write the Library of Congress, Division for the Blind and Physically Handicapped, 1291 Taylor Street, N.W., Washington, D.C. 20542.

© 1976 by American Heritage Publishing Co., Inc. All rights reserved under Berne and Pan-American Copyright Conventions. Reproduction in whole or in part of any article without permission is prohibited. Printed in the United States of America.

Brave New (*Crowded*) World

In 1776 the Lottery Magazine *of London looked toward the troublesome American colonies and—drawing on American writers including the celebrated Dr. Franklin—got off this remarkable census forecast. The tabulated figures in the second column run surprisingly close to actual U.S. census figures; for example, in 1790 the real number was 3,929,000; in 1820, 9,638,000; in 1840, 17,069,000; in 1870, 39,818,000; in 1890, 62,948,000. This accuracy fails after 1890, when the figures projected by the* Lottery *pundits are too large; but they do hedge their bet by suggesting, in their last paragraph, that "vast luxury and debauchery" in the twentieth century might cut back considerably on population increase. They knew nothing, of course, about the Pill or other recent sophistications of contraceptive science; but quite possibly they would have included them under "debauchery" if they had known. Merritt Ierley, Jr., who sent us this prescient snippet, has prepared a book on the year 1776 that will soon be forthcoming from A S. Barnes & Co., Inc.*

On the *Comparative* POPULATION of AMERICA, *with* GREAT BRITAIN.

(*Extracted from different Writers.*)

THE number of people in America are suppofed to amount to 2,200,000.* We fhall not be far from the truth, if we fuppofe the total on the continent and iflands to be about two millions and a half.

Land being plenty in America and fo cheap as that a labouring man, who underftands hufbandry, can in a fhort time fave money enough to purchafe a piece of new land fufficient for a plantation, whereon he may fubfift a family. Such men are not afraid to marry; for if they even look far enough forward, to confider how their children, when grown up, are to be provided for, they fee that more land is to be had at rates equally eafy, all their circumftances confidered.

Hence marriages in America are more general, and more generally early than in Europe. And if it is reckoned there, that there is but one marriage *per annum* among an hundred perfons, perhaps we may here reckon two; and if in Europe they have but four births to a marriage (many of their marriages being late) we may here reckon eight; of which, if one half grow up, and our marriages are made, reckoning one with another, at twenty years of age, our people muft at leaft be doubled every twenty years.

There are fuppofed to be now upwards of 1,000,000 Englifh fouls in *North* America, though it is thought fcarcely eighty thoufand have been brought over fea, and yet perhaps there is not one the fewer in Britain; but rather many more, on account of the employment the colonies afford to manufactures at home. This million doubling, fuppofe, but once in twenty-five years, will in another century be more than the people of England, and the greateft number of Englifhmen will be on this fide the water.

Another Writer fays," It appears that the land on the continent, that will admit of population, is above 1,122,800 fquare miles; and as there are 640 acres in a fquare mile, in North America we have 718,592,000 acres. England is peopled nearly in proportion of one perfon to five acres:—our colonies, fo populous, would contain 143,718,400 people. And if they contain at prefent 2,000,000, and double their numbers every twenty-five years, the period of their number will be as follows:

In 1792, they will be	-	4,000,000
1817	- - -	8,000,000
1842	- - -	16,000,000
1867	- -	32,000,000
1892	- -	64,000,000
1917	- -	128,000,000
1942	- -	256,000,000

There are feveral obftacles, however, to their encreafing in future periods at the rate they do at prefent A large proportion of them will be fixed at fo great diftance from the frefh land, (the only caufe of their quick increafe) that the difficulty of getting at it will prove an obftruction to population Great cities will be raifed among them; vaft luxury and debauchery will reign in thefe, the influence of which will extend to the extremities of the empire: and thefe caufes, which certainly will operate, muft render their increafe flower in a diftant period than it is at prefent."

---

* This was written feveral years ago, by Dr. Franklin of America.

AMERICAN HERITAGE

The Magazine of History

Sponsored by
American Association for State & Local History • Society of American Historians

CONTENTS February, 1976 Volume XXVII, Number 2

EDITOR IN CHIEF: Oliver Jensen
EDITOR: E. M. Halliday
MANAGING EDITOR: Nat Brandt
ART DIRECTOR: Emma Landau

ASSOCIATE EDITORS
Barbara Klaw   Richard F. Snow

PICTURE EDITORS
Carla Davidson   Mary Dawn Earley

COPY EDITOR: Anne D. Steinhardt
EDITORIAL ASSISTANT: Janet P. Levitt

CONSULTING EDITORS
Joan Paterson Kerr   Allan L. Damon

CONTRIBUTING EDITORS
Robert C. Alberts   Robert S. Gallagher
Richard M. Ketchum   Bernard A. Weisberger

ADVISORY BOARD
Carl Carmer, Gerald Carson,
Henry Steele Commager,
Marshall B. Davidson, John A. Garraty,
Eric F. Goldman, Louis C. Jones,
Alvin M. Josephy, Jr., Howard H. Peckham,
Francis S. Ronalds

AMERICAN HERITAGE PUBLISHING CO., INC.

SENIOR EDITORS
Bruce Catton   Joseph J. Thorndike

EDITORIAL ART DIRECTOR
Murray Belsky

PARIS OFFICE: Gertrudis Feliu
LONDON OFFICE: Christine Sutherland

AMERICAN HERITAGE is published every two months by American Heritage Publishing Co., Inc.; editorial and executive offices, 1221 Ave. of the Americas, New York, N.Y. 10020. Secretary, William Cusick. Correspondence about subscriptions should go to American Heritage Subscription Office, 383 West Center St., Marion, Ohio 43302. Single copies: $6. Annual subscriptions: $24 in U.S. and Canada; $26 elsewhere. A ten-year Index of Volumes VI-XV is available at $7.50; five-year Index of Volumes XVI-XX at $7.50; five-year Index of Volumes XXI-XXV at $7.50.

AMERICAN HERITAGE considers but assumes no responsibility for unsolicited materials; these require return postage. Title registered U.S. Patent Office. Second-class postage paid at New York, N.Y., and at additional mailing offices.

BEFORE THE COLORS FADE
PROFILE OF A SOLDIER: MATTHEW B. RIDGWAY *by Robert C. Alberts* . 4

I REMEMBER
ED: A BLACK SHARECROPPER'S STORY *drawn from interviews with Jane Maguire* 8

THE BATTLE OF LAKE ERIE *by Richard F. Snow* 14

THE STORY OF THE CENTURY *by David Davidson* 22
A close-up view of the Lindbergh kidnapping case

JOHNS HOPKINS *by Caroline Jones Franz* 30
How a great medical school began

MEN OF THE REVOLUTION XVI—DANIEL MORGAN *by Richard M. Ketchum* 34

AMERICAN HERITAGE BOOK SELECTION
PRELUDE TO WAR: THE SLAUGHTER OF THE BUFFALO *by James L. Haley* 36

TRUE LOVE WILL OUT 42

MALLET, CHISEL, AND CURLS *by Stephen W. Stathis and Lee Roderick* . . 44
Vinnie Ream, who at nineteen sculptured Lincoln

THE DON QUIXOTE OF OPERA *by Harold C. Schonberg* 48
Max Maretzek, impresario extraordinary

ARTISTS OF THE SANTA FE 57
An unusual portfolio of western painting

POSTSCRIPTS TO HISTORY 103

COVER: Under the steady glare of the southwestern sun, Indians work on a sand painting. Frederic Kimball Mizen (1888–1965), who ran a summer art school in Taos, New Mexico, painted this quiet scene. Mizen is one of the many artists represented in the Santa Fe railroad's extraordinary collection of southwestern art, from which we present a portfolio starting on page 57. The front cover of this issue of AMERICAN HERITAGE, incidentally, is the first of a new design intended to give a more varied look suggestive of the broad scope of the contents. *Back cover:* At the turn of the century, the Father of His Country's visage was always a sure bet to sell a product, whether it was tobacco or agricultural machinery. This exhalation of cigar bands is from the Walter Weichsel Cigar Band Collection in the Metropolitan Museum of Art.

BEFORE THE COLORS FADE

Profile of a Soldier:

Matthew B. Ridgway

By ROBERT C. ALBERTS

Some time ago our contributing editor Robert C. Alberts asked General Matthew B. Ridgway if he would consent to be interviewed for the AMERICAN HERITAGE series "Before the Colors Fade." The idea of the series is to record the impressions and comments of certain Americans whose careers have been so distinguished as to become a significant part of American history in their own lifetimes. General Ridgway, formerly supreme commander in the Far East and Europe, chief of staff of the United States Army, and before that a famous hero of both World War II and the Korean War, seemed a likely figure for the series; but although he agreed to answer Mr. Alberts' questions, he asked that the interview not be published as such. He feels, he says, that the question-and-answer format inevitably makes the interviewed person seem too self-centered. As a compromise we have in this instance departed from our usual policy of not running regular articles about still-living individuals. The following profile of General Ridgway is based on a number of conversations, plus a study by Mr. Alberts of the general's published work, of other articles written about him over the years, and of letters, documents, and scrapbooks he has made available. —*The Editors*

General Matthew B. Ridgway marked his eightieth birthday on March 3, 1975. He has a remarkable physique, vitality, and range of interests and activities for a man who has turned fourscore. His health is excellent except for recurrent spasms from a sacroiliac injury he sustained (and concealed) when, as a cadet at West Point, he was thrown from a horse. He is active as a director of a nonprofit foundation, of the Carnegie Hero Commission, and of Colt Industries, Inc., whose stock, he points out, has remained steady and only 5 per cent of whose business is in sales of arms to the government. He carries on an extensive correspondence with old army friends (e.g., Generals Omar Bradley, J. Lawton Collins, James Gavin), associates in government (George Ball, Robert Lovett, Cyrus R. Vance, Clark Clifford, Averell Harriman), and historians (Forrest C. Pogue, the late Cornelius Ryan). He writes an occasional article (*Foreign Affairs*, the *New York Times* Op-Ed page, the military journals). He declines all speaking engagements except an occasional appearance at the War Colleges, where he responds to questions. He and his wife live in Fox Chapel, a wooded suburb of Pittsburgh, where he was for five years chairman and chief executive officer of the country's oldest industrial-research organization.

Despite a gentle and considerate manner not always found in four-star generals, Ridgway flushes with indignation when he speaks on three subjects. One is General Sir Douglas Haig's pointless sacrifice of tens of thousands of British troops in the Passchendaele offensive in the summer and early fall of 1917. Another is General Eisenhower's conduct in 1952 when he appeared without protest on a campaign platform with Senator Joseph McCarthy, who in a three-hour Senate speech had attacked General George C. Marshall with what Ridgway calls "scurrilous and indefensible remarks whose evil effects persist to this day." The third is the studied rudeness to which he was sometimes subjected when, as army chief of staff, he dealt with Secretary of Defense Charles E. "Engine Charlie" Wilson.

Matthew Bunker Ridgway was born in 1895 at Fort Monroe, Virginia, the son of a regular army artillery colonel who had served with an international contingent in the Boxer Rebellion. He was graduated from the United States Military Academy in 1917, two of his classmates being Mark Wayne Clark and Joseph Lawton Collins. He was assigned to the infantry ("It never occurred to me to choose any other service") and served his first tour of duty as a company commander at Camp Eagle Pass, Texas, on the Mexican border. Then followed two decades of typical up-the-ladder peacetime service, with its frequent shifting

General Matthew B. Ridgway in the library of his home near Pittsburgh in 1975. Behind him is a photo of his son as a U.S. Ranger.
PHOTO BY BEN SPIEGEL

5

from place to place, its rotation among staff work, field command, schools, and diplomatic-military assignments, and its long waits for promotion (seventeen years to reach the permanent grade of major). After six years as an instructor at West Point, during which he taught Spanish and was in charge of athletics, he had fifteen assignments in seventeen years: Fort Benning; a troop command in North China with Marshall; troop service at Fort Sam Houston in San Antonio; Nicaragua; Bolivia; Fort Benning again; Nicaragua again; troop duty again in the Panama Canal Zone; the Philippines as military adviser to Governor Theodore Roosevelt, Jr.; the Command and General Staff School at Leavenworth (two years); Sixth Corps Area and Second Army headquarters in Chicago; the Army War College in Washington (one year); the Presidio in San Francisco; Brazil with Marshall; the War Plans Division back in Washington. Americans customarily kick their military around between wars; it is part of the American system. In 1941–45 that system produced a remarkable body of army commanders, some of them now almost legendary figures, and they outfought, outthought, and outgeneraled the best career professionals put in the field by enemies in Europe and Asia.

Ridgway left Washington again to take a field officer's refresher course in Fort Benning, arriving there on a notable Sunday morning—December 7, 1941. A few months later, with the nation at war, he succeeded Omar Bradley as a two-star general in command of the reactivated 82nd Infantry Division. When a special messenger from Washington asked Ridgway: "How would you like to turn this division into an airborne outfit?" he replied: "I've never heard of one, but I would be happy to do it." He hied himself to Fort Benning and—at age forty-seven—made his first parachute jump to see what it was like. To his dubious infantrymen he said: "It was the most glorious feeling in the world. You feel like the lord of creation floating way up above the earth." He did not dwell on his first landing, which he says was like jumping off the top of a moving freight car onto a hard clay roadbed. On May 10, 1943, he and his division, now the 82nd Airborne, disembarked at Casablanca and resumed their training operations in fields around Oujda in Morocco.

The Germans had made the first large-scale parachute and glider assault in taking Crete from the British in May, 1941, with casualties so heavy that they never again tried such an operation. The second large assault, and the first large night drop in history, was made by part of the 82nd Airborne Division in the Sicily campaign on July 10, 1943, three hours before the beach assault. Ridgway went ashore from General Patton's command ship and proceeded inland on foot with a sergeant and an aide to find his troopers, set up a command post, and get on with the business of helping to clean up the western end of the island. The 2nd Armored Division was assigned to take Palermo, but when its tank patrols roared into the town square, they were applauded derisively by 82nd Division paratroopers who had been there for some time.

The airdrop in Sicily had serious defects: the twenty-eight hundred troopers had been too widely dispersed, and there were other errors that cost lives. But the drop served its purpose by disrupting and delaying German reinforcements that might have dislodged the beachhead. "From that time forward," Ridgway says,

> every higher commander felt he had a new tactical weapon to call upon: vertical envelopment. Was there an enemy strong point to be assaulted? Drop a battalion of paratroopers on it. Was it an especially difficult objective that called for a major effort? Send in several regiments of troopers and follow next morning with the gliders. This was the exciting, dashing, progressive way to defeat the enemy.
>
> I heard or saw about a dozen major tactical plans in the Italian mainland campaign, and I can't recall one of them that did not include some mission for airborne troops—which at that time generally meant me and my 82nd Airborne.
>
> The trouble was, higher tactical commanders at that time had some inappropriate ideas on what constituted a suitable mission. They had little comprehension of the complexities of an airborne operation or of its limitations once the unit was on the ground.
>
> I understood the limitations of my division, and my staff understood them. We knew how complicated an airborne operation could be, especially one carried out at night. It requires almost perfect coordination between fighting aircraft, transport planes and gliders, men on the ground, and off-lying naval vessels. Even a perfect drop will have errors that would be disastrous to a fighting unit not trained to overcome them. The troopers will be scattered over many square miles of strange enemy territory, and until they can "roll up the stick," they must act alone or in small groups. When the fighting begins, they are almost always in a situation that would spell catastrophe to most other units: they are completely surrounded by the enemy.
>
> Once it has landed, an airborne division fights under conditions that would be unacceptable to any infantry unit other than a Ranger battalion. If it is not supplied, it is finished as a fighting force, since it cannot move back toward a supply base. At the time of the Italian campaign we could not drop a jeep or an armored car. The heaviest airdrop then feasible by parachute was the barrel of the 75-mm pack howitzer, which weighed about three hundred pounds. The carriage had to be dropped separately. Even then the weapon was ineffective against tanks. Today ten-thousand-pound

CONTINUED ON PAGE 73

Ridgway en route: Upper left, with his mother and father at Fort Andrews, Massachusetts, 1912; center, as a young infantry officer returning from Nicaragua in 1930; upper right, conferring with Major General James M. Gavin somewhere in Belgium in 1945; left center, posing in February, 1945, with other Western Front generals (left to right: Eisenhower; Courtney H. Hodges; Clarence R. Huebner; Edwin P. Parker, hatless; Omar N. Bradley); right center, with Field Marshal Bernard Montgomery, 1945; lower left, visiting troops in Korea, March, 1951; lower right, touring the Korean front with General Douglas MacArthur in January, 1951.

7

I REMEMBER

ED
A Black Sharecropper's Story

DRAWN FROM INTERVIEWS WITH JANE MAGUIRE

When Ed Brown finally left Abbeville, Georgia, in 1962, he and his wife worked as domestics for Jane Maguire's family, first in Atlanta and then for thirteen years in New York City. During those years Ms. Maguire became fascinated by Ed's sharp memories of what life was like for a black farmhand in Georgia, and she persuaded him—he is illiterate—to let her help tell his story. She interviewed him, taking careful notes over a period of about four years, and assembled the interviews into a consecutive reminiscence entitled simply Ed. His direct, unself-pitying, and often heartbreaking story will be published by W. W. Norton later this month, and we are pleased to publish the following excerpt from this unusual memoir.

Mr. Brown is now retired and lives in Brooklyn, New York, where his two daughters by a second marriage are in high school.

ON SHARES

In 1929 Mr. Addison bought a tractor. He was the first man I ever knowed to have one. Right away he cut the fifteen men on his place down to four hands. It would be a favor to him, he say, if I could get myself another job. That was the turrible year I worked on shares for Mr. Leslie Prince.

To buy food and to take care of the smokin and chewin me and my wife wanted to do while we was makin the crop, Mr. Prince said he'd loan me ten dollars a month. He would put it out, he say, but not all in cash, January through June, with interest at 15 per cent. He was aimin to make me take all the meat and syrup he could from his smokehouse.

Then, on shares, the boss furnish you with the land, mule, seeds, tools, and one half of the fertilizer. I was to put out the other half of the fertilizer and all the labor.

Things went all right for a while. I was the best cotton picker there. Whenever Mr. Prince hire anyone to pick by the hundredweight, he said, "I want you to beat Ed pickin." The most I ever picked in an hour was a hundred and thirty-five pounds.

But hard work didn't get me nowhere. Mr. Prince wouldn't show me the papers the gin and the warehouse give him, so I didn't know what the crop had brung and what my share should be. He took his share and all of mine and claim I owe him twenty-four dollars in addition.

In panic times ten dollars would buy a horse wagon full of groceries. You could buy ten pounds of sugar for fifty cents, fifteen pounds of bacon for ten or fifteen cents a pound. A gallon of syrup would cost fifty cents, and so would a peck sack of flour.

And usually I had a garden, either for myself or on halves with the boss, such as potatoes, squashes, onions, turnips, collards, cabbage, snap beans, butter beans, peas, Irish potatoes, tomatoes, and okra. Come summer my wife would put up seventy-five or eighty jars of blackberries, plums, watermelon rinds, apple preserves, and jelly. She raised chickens, and I would have a sweet-potato patch

Robert Gwathmey, a white Southerner by birth, is a painter who has always felt particular empathy toward black subjects. His simple and evocative serigraph, "Share Croppers," was made in 1939.
PRIVATE COLLECTION

COPYRIGHT © 1976 BY JANE MAGUIRE

and a cane patch.

After the ten-dollars-a-month furnish money was cut off in June, it was best to be with a fellow that knowed you had to live through the winter too. A landlord would most likely want you and your family to have enough to eat if you was stayin on to make another crop. But if you wasn't, he didn't care.

My wife want us to work for Mr. Prince because his tenant house had glass windows. When he come by our house, he would smile and wave, wave and smile. She say, "I declare that is a nice man. I believe he would be a good man to work for."

I thought it would suit me because he said I could make a garden on halves. Before I had gathered much, Mr. Prince acted friendly to some people: "Get anythin out of the garden you want." They cleaned it out. That made me a little dissatisfied. And my wife kicked because whenever I want to borrow Mr. Prince's mule to carry her to church on Sunday, he would say, "No, the mule should rest on Sunday."

Another reason I was dissatisfied was because I was a strong man behind a goin mule. Mr. Prince figure my time worth the same as one of his boys. They was chillen at the time, and quite natural they couldn't do a man's work.

Most white chillen went to school. But any landlord who was furnishin money to feed a colored tenant would expect him to take his chillen out of school to do what need doin on the farm.

By walkin over the farm all the time Mr. Prince knowed if you was behind with anythin. After school and on Saturday he had his sons work for me. "Ed, what about takin the chillen over there to soda your cotton?"

The boys would walk over thirty acres of cotton carryin a one-half-gallon bucket of soda in one hand and droppin it with the other. I'd follow along behind plowin the soda under. Whatever time the chillen spent helpin me I'd owe their daddy. I didn't favor that.

After a year's hard work and makin a good crop I ask Mr. Prince for a settlement. "I ain't got the books ready today," he said. "I want to have a settlement when we get through gatherin everythin." After I had even my late corn in the crib, I went back and he got out the book.

It didn't look to me like he could figure worth nothin—'bout like me. I had made seven bales of cotton and two horse wagon loads of corn, but Mr. Prince claim I hadn't made enough to pay off my sixty dollars' furnish money and that I still owed him twenty-four dollars.

He put the corn in the crib without weighin it. Velvet beans was bringin a dollar a hundred pounds, and he took all of them. And all the sweet potatoes.

"I tell you what I'm goin to do," he say. "I'll take your milk cow for the twenty-four dollars."

Me and my wife had brung the cow and the calf I swapped for my Model T Ford with us from the Addison place. We brung two hogs, and I had give Mr. Prince one to let me fatten the other in the peanut field. He took both of them.

"No, I'm not givin the milk cow, because it don't belong to me, it belong to my wife."

"Well, you could just give me a mortgage on the cow and carry her on with you."

I goes home and tell my wife, "Don't give no mortgage on the cow. Don't give nothin on her."

My wife was more nervy about some things than I was. She put a rope around the cow's neck and carry her to my brother's. Then she make another trip there with the two little pigs she got washin and ironin for her boss lady. Mr. Prince took my pig he was lettin me fatten in his peanut field.

I goes back to him. He was settin on the steps to his porch. "Mr. Prince, it don't look to me I owe you that much, not twenty-four dollars."

He had give his boy a long knife. "David, bring me the knife," he say.

I walk on off. After that he just kept a comin to my house late at night, way in the night, and wantin me to go out in the field with him "to talk it over."

"How come you can't talk it over here to the house? We ain't got to go in the field to talk over no settlement. I didn't come to your house late in the night to get this place."

"We'll go out where it cool."

"It cool enough for me in here."

I seed there wasn't no use talkin. If it had been fair as a lily and he'd said it was rainin and I'd said no, he'd said I was disputin his word. And if you had met him, you'd a thought he was the best man in the world. He wouldn't pass colored or white except he'd speak and smile, speak and smile.

He'd go to the table every mornin and say a long prayer over it, and then he'd come right out of that house and take every bit of bread out of your mouth. And he'd raise more sand than forty lawyers. "Now, I'm goin to the field, boys, and it'll pay you all to come on." He'd plow until about eleven and then quit. "You colored can stand the sun."

When it come a big rain, he'd say, "Boys, let's get the cross saw and cut stovewood." I had a pile of stovewood I don't know how high in the yard. So did the other tenants and Mr. Prince. He'd get his wood cut that a way without payin for it.

One mornin come a rain. "Let's cut some stovewood."

I say, "I ain't cuttin nare nother stick of stovewood for nobody. I've got enough stovewood to last me. What I'm worried about is gettin somethin to cook with this I got."

After that I'd walk about when it was rainin. He talked around. "Well, Ed's a good hand, but he sure is mean." I wasn't mean. I just wasn't goin to cut no more stovewood. When you got enough of anythin, you don't need no more.

When I was fixin to leave, Mr. Prince ask me, "Ed, have you found a place to live?"

"Yes, sir, up there with Mr. Motley."

"Motley at Rochelle?"

"Yes, sir."

I went to Mr. Motley to get his wagon to move. "I think our deal is off, Ed. Mr. Leslie Prince just been here, and he say you're a good hand but you're mean and your wife is sick and your little girl is too small to do anythin."

I didn't know what to do. I had stayed in my place and lived in my bounds. You had to be mighty sharp then to make it for your folks. Mighty sharp and straight humble. If you wasn't, it'd make you have ulcers. You could get 'em from bein humble and from not bein humble enough.

One thing you was workin for was so the white man would say, "He's a good nigger." Then the others would let you alone. If one say you steal, whether you steal or not, if somethin is missin you took it.

Things was burdenin me. I walked back from Mr. Motley's towards Mr. Prince's. When I come to the black gum tree which was still scarred up from a lynchin that took place when I was a boy, I set down to study this thing out. The trouble was I hadn't left Mr. Prince when his other two tenants left. They was smarter than me.

When one of them see what our boss was like, him and his wife and two chillen cleared out just before layin-by time, about July 4. Me and Emmett, the other tenant, was in the barn. Mr. Prince come by and say, "That lazy nigger is leavin. If anybody else want to go, they're at liberty." The tenant leavin told us he suspicion the boss's bookkeepin. He went to pickin cotton by the hundredweight and made money.

Emmett stay till the cotton all picked and the corn gathered and we was bailin hay. It was the last of October when him and Mr. Prince fell out. We had finished everythin but strippin cane. "Ed, if you'll stay," Mr. Prince say, "I'll give you what I been aimin to give you and both the others."

He didn't give me nothin but plenty of trouble. I reckon that's what he was goin to give them and he decide he'd give it all to me.

It took me two days to strip the cane and take it to the mill. All one day I chopped the wood for cookin it. So that was three days' work. Mr. Prince wasn't promisin me money for helpin with the cane, but I was supposed to get half the syrup.

I was just beginnin the fourth day's work when a colored gentleman, a butcher, come out from Rochelle and bought a cow. He had got old. If I help him butcher this cow, he'll give me the tripe, the head, the tail, and the feets. So I goes to Mr. Prince. It was early in the mornin, and he was at the table prayin. I had to wait the longest for him to get through; then I ask him could I help butcher the cow. "Go if you want to."

After we butcher the cow, I jump over the fence and taken what meat the butcher give me to my wife. We was glad to get it. Then I goes right back to the sugar mill and ask Mr. Prince what do he want me to do. "Nothin, you quit and went to helpin somebody else."

He had promised to pay me in syrup. Now he didn't want me to have any. So I ask him to pay me in money. He turnt me off. I ask him to let me cut him a cord of wood for an overall jacket to wear the comin winter. "No. I don't need no wood cut. I can tie a string around my plantation, and me and my boys can live in it for twelve months."

The way I look at it, all our work—mine and the other tenants'—was piled up around him.

Soon after that we left there. My wife was singin and bouncin Lottie on her knees.

Ought's a ought,
All for the white man
None for the nigger.

PANIC TIME

Durin the worst of the panic people was walkin to and fro, up and down the highway. Men would come into the settlement and go from house to house beggin for somethin, anythin to do. The white people could get a yard cut for thirty cents and hedges clipped for twenty-five cents.

In 1930 I sold my cotton for five cents a pound. My share of that was two and a half cents. A man who didn't have no regular way of gettin food had to steal or starve.

Bob Abbott couldn't get a farm. Him and his wife and chillen—five or six—didn't have enough to eat. I come acrost him one day settin on the railroad.

"How is your people?"

"Down with the measles."

"What you settin here for?"

"I'm scared of the measles."

But he caught them and died. While he was livin him and his people went hungry. But the day he died I went by the leakin, broken-down house he was livin in, and you couldn't hardly get in his yard for the people bringin ham, shoulders, flour, meal. It was all stacked up.

Just about the time of the panic the tractor come in strong. At first it didn't have rubber tires, just cleats that would catch in the ground. The driver would only work in the middle of the field, and men with mules went in the corners and along the fences, where you couldn't turn a tractor around.

In just a few years the tractor improved so much it put the mule out of business. The landowner was quick to take a likin to the tractor. With it he would have no people to feed, no doctors' bills or houses to repair, and no mules to feed. He could buy fertilizer with the money he used to pay hands.

Men started walkin the roads lookin for a farm, for a dry place to sleep, and a place to raise somethin to eat. Mr. So and So, they'd tell me, has got a tractor and I got to move. Some would walk weeks lookin for a farm.

One day my granddaughter answer a knock at the back door. "It's a white man out there!" She run to me when she seed him.

I goes to find what do he want. Together with him bein white, what scared my granddaughter, I think, is that he was bearded and had a long, poor face. Do we have any food to give him? "How many eggs can he eat?" my wife ask.

"About seven."

She cook them and fry him some bacon and make him some hot biscuits and a pot of coffee. I put a quart of buttermilk in front of him. There was syrup and butter on the table. He finished every bit of it. Then he come and set down in the front room. "If I had a place to lay down now and go to sleep, I'd be all right."

I was afraid to keep him.

We was havin a dry spell and I had been haulin water from Abbeville, where he come from. I decided to haul water from Rochelle because if I carry him there, he wouldn't be passin by my house again.

An old, old gentleman come one cold winter night. He was raggedty and patched every which a way. After he got thawed out by the fire, he was settin there talkin. I ask him where was he travelin to.

"Florida."

"Why you walkin way to Florida?"

"The one I love is down there and I'm goin to get married."

"Married?"

"Yeah."

"Well, I believe if I had got as old as you is, I wouldn't take a wife."

"Yeah, all of them tell me that. But they just like you."

"How's that?"

"They're settin up side of theirs."

One day in Hoover times comin home from Kramer along the railway track, I walk up on a fellow sittin in a dugout.

He was travelin to Savannah, and I say, "I'm goin on down about a mile. We can walk along together." He was carryin a bundle of clothes tied up in a bed sheet. When we got nearly to the turnoff for my place, we come on a dead rabbit the train had run over. The man grabbed this rabbit just like it had been alive and was goin to run.

I tell him to my knowin the dead rabbit had been there for three days, if not longer.

He helt it up and smelt it. "That ain't nothin," he say. "It ain't ruint. It will help me travel."

When he got to the railway trestle, he stop and wash the rabbit, and I reckon he eat it, because when I left he was buildin a fire.

One Saturday about ten or twelve men, white and colored, was workin on my place with the peanut picker. We didn't get through until near sundown. I had about four tons of hay to haul in before the rain come. "Who will help me haul in my hay?"

All of them holler, "Not me, not me."

A white man named George spoke. "I will," he say. The next mornin before day he come back with a truck and woke me up. "I'm ready to help you." By eight o'clock that mornin we had it all in. I paid him five dollars.

Him and his wife busted up, and he leave and stay off one or two years. Then one night about twelve o'clock someone knock and call my name.

"Who is it?" I ask.

"George. Don't you know I help you haul in your hay that Sunday mornin?"

I open the door.

He told me to get up and make a fire. Me and him set and talk. He told about drivin a big transfer truck haulin produce from Florida to Atlanta and how he was goin to bring me some beans. I was settin up there believin him. Once I ask did he want to take off the overcoat he was wearin, and he say no.

"Ed, would you give me a quilt and let me stretch out here in front of the fire?" I didn't hurry about answerin, and he brung up the hay again. "You know I did you a favor."

The colored didn't go to the white and the white didn't go to the colored to spend the night. I ask myself why he doin it. I give him the quilt.

My wife say, "If you go to sleep, I'll stay woke."

We both go to sleep. When we knowed anythin it was day. I built another fire. Soon as he woke, George say, "Let's go down to the barn." We walk out there. "Ed, I been tellin you a bunch of stories. The reason I had to tell you that, I didn't want your family to be scared. I want you to do me a favor."

"What is it?" I ask.

"I want you to pull off your clothes and give them to me. This is a right new suit I got on. If you can get the letters out of it, you can wear it; if you can't, burn it up and get shut of it."

He pull off his coat. He was wearin a gray khaki chain-gang suit.

"I'll try to find you some." So I goes to the house and get my one white shirt and my one pair of Sunday pants. I tell him, "Put this on." He change into my clothes and come back to the house to wash his face and comb his hair.

He look nice.

"In two weeks' time you'll hear from me." I never have.

Helpin your neighbors was different. One lady thank me still. Her husband runned away and lef her with three chillen. Out in the country sometimes it was hard for a lady to get a job. A lot of the white people cook for theyselves.

The last time I seed this lady, she grab me and hug me and told some of 'em at the Piney Grove church homecomin, "This man helped me when I couldn't help myself. He let me have food out of his garden and out of his kitchen to feed my chillen, and I love him for it."

In panic times if you couldn't get a job and make enough to feed yourself and them in your family not able to work, you'd have to figure another way to live.

McLeod was a born burglar. He would steal the sweetnin out of a ginger cake or a thing so minor you wouldn't miss it, but as he got it he'd carry it across the road and give it to someone there.

If there was somethin particular you didn't want him to take, it was best to say so.

We had about seventy-five chickens my wife had raised that bunched theyselves up on the east side of the house in the shade. One time me and my wife come back from town and driv up in our yard, and there was McLeod settin on the porch lookin at the chickens.

Since Mac was a known chicken thief, I walk right straight to him. "Don't bother my wife's chickens."

"Well, I'm glad you told me not to get them, because I was just thinkin about sackin them up."

"I'll help you out any way I can if you don't bother them."

That night he went to his mother-in-law's chicken house and help hisself to as many as he could get in two big sacks without smotherin them. Some of them was stickin they heads out of the holes he had cut in the sacks.

The next mornin he come to my house and 'minded me I say I'd help him. I took him in my wagon to Rochelle, where he try to sell them chickens on the street. Some he took ten, fifteen, or twenty cents apiece for.

How come he to sell them so cheap was because they was frizzly chickens—with feathers curly like a curly-headed man. When they young, they look very pretty with curly feathers all over, but they molt and get to look near about half naked.

They scratch a lot. I always said they was scratchin for a livin. But many folks claim they was very good for scratchin up a conjuration somebody had put down in your yard.

Frizzly chickens is no different from any other chickens once you get the feathers off. But people don't like to eat them. Even at such a cheap price Mac was told, "I don't want them buzzards."

Mac come to spend two or three days with his sister so he could see what his brother-in-law, Rogers Hollis, had. The main thing was one milk cow. Mac got some men's shoes and ties them on the cow's feet so Rogers won't be able to follow her tracks. After Mac lead the cow to the railway tracks, he take off the shoes and walk her from Burnham's Bay to Vienna, Georgia, about twenty miles.

He goes to the hands on a big farm. They was goin to buy the cow for seven dollars and butcher it and divide the beef amongst them. But before they could make up the money, the law come and arrest McLeod. The judge sentence him to twelve months. If he didn't steal somethin from jail, I would be surprised.

After Mac was in jail awhile, Mr. Hyatt Wilcox paid his fine and got him out. Mr. Wilcox would not pay him in cash but let him take up his wages in groceries at the store.

Saturday night Mac was in the habit of takin up enough groceries for two or three people. Then he'd go right out behind the store and sell what he'd got for cash. If he had took up one dollar's worth of groceries, he'd sell them for fifty cents or even twenty-five. After pilin up a big debt at the store he runned away.

The first I knowed McLeod was back, my brother driv up to my house and call, "Hey, Ed, here Mac! He want me to carry him over to Miss Estelle's." That was his mother-in-law. "You want to go with us?" I was settin in the bathtub and told them no. It was Saturday evenin, and he had slipped back on the Seaboard train that run through there then to see his wife.

Somehow the white folks got in the winds of McLeod bein back. I was livin on Mr. Addison's place in Kramer in a house that white people had once lived in. It had glass windows and a narrow porch with a rail that run acrost the front of it.

About midnight there was a knock at the door. Whoever was there had come up quiet. I look out the front window. There was two men settin on the rail. I walk into the dinin room, where my two sisters was settin up in bed. "What is you done?"

"Nothin," they both say. I look out the dinin room window and there was men in the yard.

I want to tell you the honest truth; that's a turrible feelin to be surrounded like that. There was one or two men at every crack that open out my house. In them days the whites would come and take people out and try to whup 'em, beat 'em to death, kill 'em. I didn't want that to happen. I had always said if the whites ever come there at me, I'm goin to make them kill me right there in front of my folks and not way off somewhere. Now I couldn't figure what to do.

I walk into my bedroom. "What is you done?" My wife was drawed up under the covers cryin and prayin.

"I ain't done nothin." When I look out the bedroom

CONTINUED ON PAGE 91

The Battle of Lake Erie

*"With half the western world at stake,
See Perry on the middle lake."*
—Nineteenth-century ballad

Two years after the battle the sailing master of the schooner Ariel, *Thomas Brownell, commissioned a relative, George I. Cook, to paint this picture of the fight. Perry himself stopped by to make suggestions while the work was in progress. The result, wrote Brownell, "is a correct representation of that naval combat, in which, for the first time in her history, Great Britain lost a whole fleet..."*

U.S. NAVAL ACADEMY MUSEUM, ANNAPOLIS

By RICHARD F. SNOW

In the late summer of 1812 a Great Lakes merchant captain named Daniel Dobbins arrived in Washington. He had had a dreadful time getting there, and his journey could not have been made more pleasant by the fact that he was bringing some very bad news with him.

On July 12, a month after President Madison announced a state of war between the United States and Great Britain, General William Hull had invaded Canada with twenty-two hundred men. Hull issued a number of sententious proclamations about the liberty and prosperity that would follow in the wake of his invasion, and then almost immediately quailed before minor British resistance and false reports of large numbers of the enemy nearby. By August 8 Hull was back in Detroit, where, a week later, he surrendered all his troops and his well-supplied garrison to a force half the size of his, composed mainly of militia and Indians. Whatever the reason for Hull's extraordinary performance—it was variously ascribed to cowardice, senility, and treason—his capitulation left the American Northwest in the control of the British and Daniel Dobbins a prisoner.

This was particularly bad luck for Dobbins, for he was believed by his captors to have violated an earlier parole. He was told that he was to be executed but escaped from the British camp in a thunderstorm. A reward was offered for his scalp, and so, having anticipated this, he hid in a wrecked boat on the shore of the Detroit River. At length he made for the river's mouth, where he found an abandoned Indian dugout. He paddled across Lake Erie to Sandusky and there got hold of a horse, which he rode to Cleveland. Then, again in a canoe, he pressed on to the harbor of Presque Isle—which was beginning to be known as the town of Erie—where the officer in command of a small blockhouse told him to carry his doleful news to Washington. So Dobbins travelled the long, dangerous forest road to Pittsburgh and then headed east.

Soon after he finally reached the capital, he was taken before President Madison, who immediately summoned a cabinet meeting to discuss Dobbins' news. At the very beginning of the war Madison had hoped to take Canada by invasion, thereby obviating the need for a costly American fleet on the Lakes. Now Hull's defeat had shown him that such a fleet was indispensable. Dobbins must have given a good account of himself, since Madison turned to him for advice. What did the lake captain think was the best place for building a fleet on Lake Erie? Dobbins recommended Presque Isle and was promptly given the service rank of sailing master and orders to proceed to Erie and build a flotilla.

However well Dobbins may have impressed the rattled Madison, it is unlikely that he would have been given his post had not Lake Erie seemed something of a side show. The President, quite reasonably, expected the real contest to take place on Lake Ontario, for Ontario dominated all the supply routes from the St. Lawrence to the upper Lakes. Although there was no American navy at all on Erie, there was already one of sorts on Ontario, its mainstay a sixteen-gun brig. Across the lake, operating out of Kingston Harbor, was a British fleet mounting upward of seventy guns. It was clear then that a first-rate commander was needed to seize the advantage on Lake Ontario. So the Navy Department gave the crucial command of the naval forces on Lakes Ontario and Erie to Isaac Chauncey.

Chauncey was an irritable, vigorous, corpulent man who had commanded his first ship when he was just nineteen. Now he was forty years old, a well-respected veteran of the Tripolitan war, where his courage under fire had drawn a special commendation from the exacting Commodore Preble. After the war he spent a year's furlough from the Navy as captain of a ship belonging to John Jacob Astor and then returned to the service to take command of the Brooklyn Navy Yard. On September 3 of 1812 he was called from this last duty to go to the Lakes; and by the end of the month, when he embarked on an antediluvian steamboat for the twenty-hour trip to Albany, he had already sent north scores of soldiers, sailors, and ship carpenters. He seemed to be the perfect man for the job.

Dobbins was also heading north late in September. His destination, Presque Isle, was a narrow finger of land six miles long, hooked out into Lake Erie and enclosing a superb natural harbor three miles long and more than a mile wide. A sandbar across the entrance to the bay presented some difficulties, but once inside, a ship was safe from any storm that might blow up.

Aside from this harbor and the fine timber that grew all about it, there was nothing there to encourage the construction of a fleet. There were forty-seven houses in the bleak little community, one blacksmith shop, and a few men who knew how to use whipsaws. There was no metal to speak of within a hundred miles, nor was there any rope or sailcloth to be had. The only cannon in the place was a small iron boat howitzer; it had been found on the beach years before, and the villagers liked to shoot it off on the Fourth of July.

When Dobbins got to Presque Isle on September 24, he had two thousand dollars and a few carpenters with which to build a navy. Two thousand dollars wasn't very much money for the task, but Dobbins, acting on the assumption that there would be more coming, spent with a free hand. He set the price of timber at a dollar a tree. He sent to Meadville, some thirty miles away, for some steel and paid the blacksmith $2.00 a day to forge the steel into axes. Sawyers were to earn $1.25 a day and axemen 62½ cents. Hauling was worth $4.00 a day to those who had horses or oxen.

A few days after his arrival Dobbins wrote a letter to "Commodore Chauncey or the commanding officer of the lake at Buffaloe":

SIR: I have the honor to transmit to you . . . a coppy of my instructions from the Secretary of the Navy and assure you, Sir, that I stand ready to execute any orders you may be pleased to issue. . . .

Dobbins must have been infuriated by the reply that he received a few days later:

It appears to me utterly impossible to build Gun Boats at Presqu'ile; there is not a sufficient depth of water on the bar to get them into the Lake. Should there be water, the place is at all times open to the attacks of the Enemy.... From a slight acquaintance I have with our side of Lake Erie ... I am under the impression [it] has not a single Harbor calculated to fit out a Naval expedition, and the only one convenient I am at present at.... I have no further communication to make on the subject.

This frustrating message was not signed by Chauncey but by Lieutenant Jesse Duncan Elliott. Elliott, who had just turned thirty, had been sent by Chauncey to take command of operations on Lake Erie. He was a vain man, and he was a troublemaker.

Elliott's rank was superior to the one hastily conferred on Dobbins. But Dobbins knew Lake Erie; he had been sailing the Lakes for more than a decade. He was sure that he had picked the right spot in Presque Isle, and he was still very much a civilian, with a good republican mistrust of military wisdom. He wrote Elliott a testy letter explaining that he had "as perfect a knowledge of this lake as any other man on it" and went ahead with his work.

It was well that he did, for Elliott had lit on a curious spot for his operations. He was at Black Rock, near Buffalo, in a harbor so close to the British base across the Niagara at Fort Erie that soldiers frequently exchanged shots across the river. Moreover, vessels seeking the open lake would have to work their way through three miles of channels against a four-knot current right under the guns of the enemy. In this cul-de-sac Elliott had assembled a fleet of small schooners, bought up and down the lake.

Despite his dubious anchorage, however, Elliott did lead a spirited cutting-out operation a few days after he wrote his highhanded letter to Dobbins. Along with fifty sailors and fifty soldiers under Army Captain Nathan Towson, he put out from the American shore in darkness and moved against two British vessels that were riding at anchor in front of the fort. His barges were spotted from the deck of the brig *Caledonia,* but Towson scrambled aboard despite heavy musketry and managed to bring the brig—and its welcome cargo of $150,000 worth of pelts—back to Black Rock. Elliott secured the brig *Detroit* (which had been captured from Hull at Detroit) but ran her aground and, under heavy artillery fire, ordered her burned. Long afterward Towson, rankling over the scant credit that the Army received in Elliott's official report, would try to provoke him into a duel; but for the moment the country was happy with this small success, and Elliott was a hero. Congress voted him a sword, and the next summer he was promoted to master commandant, over the heads of thirty of his senior lieutenants.

Elliott had added another ship to

Perry used this house as headquarters while he built his fleet at Erie, Pennsylvania.
History of Erie County BY LAURA SANFORD, 1861

his squadron, but bottled up as it was in Black Rock, neither the *Caledonia* nor any other of his ships was of any immediate use to him.

Meanwhile, as autumn burned itself out in the forests around him, Dobbins worked to get ships by less spectacular means than splashy nighttime raids. He laid down the keels for two brigs and three gunboats. Supplies trickled in from Philadelphia, and from Pittsburgh by way of the Allegheny and French rivers. Dobbins paid one J. McDonald $200 for four foremasts, four mainmasts, four main booms, and four bowsprits. John Greenwood turned out sixty sweeps and fifty 14-foot oars for $92.25, and N. Richardson attempted to sell him the products of a "very extensive rope-walk in Kentucky." Winter blew down from the north, and one of his workers died; others began to desert. Dobbins did all he could to keep them there and all the while wrote increasingly desperate letters to Chauncey and then to the Secretary of the Navy begging for instructions:

The boats that I have laid down are 50 feet keel 17 feet beams 5 feet hold and from appearances will be fast sailors if you wish me to go on with the work you will Pleas give me orders to draw I have expended a considerable sum more than the two thousand dollars ... I have brot the iron from Pittsburgh which comes high the Roads have been so bad if I am directed to go on with the work Pleas let me hear as soon as Posible.

Chauncey maintained a monumental silence, and it seems that the Secretary of the Navy did as well. But at last, in late December, Chauncey left his base on Lake Ontario to pay a visit to Lake Erie. There he found that the carpenters who had been converting the schooners at Black Rock to naval vessels had finally been discouraged by the combination of winter and enemy musketry and had returned to New York, leaving the ships in a dismal state of disrepair. Chauncey journeyed on to Presque Isle, where he studied the harbor and decided that Dobbins had been right; it was the best place for the American navy.

Dobbins soon received assistance more material than Chauncey's approval. In January of 1813 the Navy Department sent Noah Brown, a superb New York shipbuilder, up to Lake Erie to build two large brigs. And at about the same time Oliver Hazard Perry petitioned Chauncey for a command on the Lakes.

Perry had been born twenty-seven years before in Rhode Island. Despite his family's Quaker wellsprings, his father, Christopher, had fought in the Revolution, and Oliver was wild to get to sea by the time he was thirteen. The next year his father took him in as a midshipman on his frigate, and the boy saw action in the Caribbean during the naval war with France. He served in the Mediterranean at the time of the Tripolitan war and was made an acting lieutenant in 1803 and a permanent one four years later. He spent the first two years of his lieutenancy employed in the frustrating task of building gunboats; these balky craft were part of an illusory scheme to keep the British navy from violating Jefferson's embargo. At last, in 1809, he was given command of the schooner *Revenge*. He got some creditable attention when he captured an American ship whose skipper had, in effect, stolen her from her owners and sailed her under English colors. For the most part, however, his duty was unspeakably tedious: he was to cruise up and down the Atlantic coast on the lookout for seizures of American ships by British men-of-war—which in any event the fourteen small guns of the *Revenge* would have been powerless to forestall. Even so, it was better than gunboat service. Then in January of 1811 the *Revenge*, making for New London in a thick fog, ran aground and sank. The pilot was in charge at the time, and Perry was completely exonerated at the court of inquiry that followed. Nevertheless he was dismayed to find himself back on gunboat duty, operating out of Newport. Fretful and restless, he wrote everyone he could think of, begging for a different service; and at last, a little more than a year after the loss of the *Revenge*, Chauncey petitioned for Perry to serve under him, saying that the young captain could "be employed to great advantage, particularly on Lake Erie, where I shall not be able to go so early as I expected, owing to the increasing force of the enemy on this lake."

Chauncey had made a brilliant choice, but in his petition can be read a clue to the shortcomings that would hamstring the man in his own operations on Lake Ontario. He was always haunted by the "increasing force of the enemy," and it is fortunate indeed that his English counterpart across the lake, Sir James Lucas Yeo, harbored the same fears. Yeo turned up available for duty when he lost his ship on an uncharted reef in the West Indies. The court-martial took a lenient view of his mishap and acquitted Yeo; then, for little better reason than the fact that he had lost his ship and needed a job, he was given command of the British naval forces on the Lakes.

He immediately began to build ships on Lake Ontario, and Chauncey did the same. All through the spring and summer of 1813 the balance of naval power seesawed back and forth as Yeo and Chauncey launched ever larger ships. Chauncey was a magnificent organizer; he produced a strong fleet out of raw timber in the wilderness but was always scared to fight it. And so with Yeo; he built the ships but lacked the determination to use them as they should be used. The two growing navies sparred timidly at each other and then retired to

Oliver Hazard Perry by Rembrandt Peale
NEW-YORK HISTORICAL SOCIETY

equip themselves better for the decisive action that would someday come. This shipbuilding race was carried to extremes; by the end of the war Chauncey had nearly finished building a 130-gun ship of the line, a vessel three times larger than anything America had on salt water. But by that time Perry's operations on Lake Erie had made the command of Lake Ontario seem little more than a tactical exercise.

As soon as Perry got his transfer orders from the Navy Department, he sent fifty carpenters and sailors north to Erie, and he himself set out by sleigh. He arrived at Presque Isle at dusk on March 27. Noah Brown, the New York shipbuilder, had arrived two weeks before and was there with Dobbins to greet Perry when he arrived in the haggard town. The winter had slowed construction down, but Perry found the two brigs well under way as he first examined them in the fading light.

Perry took command vigorously and at once. He sent parties out into the wilderness to scare up a detachment of carpenters that had left Philadelphia for Erie weeks before, and put pressure on the carpenters who were already there. As more straggled in the pace of work increased, although Perry never had more than two hundred men building his fleet. He was in a hurry—he wanted to get out on the lake as soon as possible—and he rushed his men. As the ships took shape it became obvious that they would bear some of the marks of hasty construction. They were made of green timber; trees that were standing in the forest at daybreak would often be part of a hull by dusk. It is said that Brown, coming upon a carpenter who was taking too much time with a particular task, said to the man: "We want no extras; plain work, plain work, is all we want. They are only required for one battle; if we win, that is all that will be wanted of them. If the enemy are victorious, the work is good enough to be captured." Wooden-peg construction was used largely in all sailing ships of the era, but the scarcity of metal forced the Erie builders to use pegs in places where nails were considered vital. There was nothing to be done about it; Perry had all he could do to scare up enough iron to make mounts for the guns.

The guns themselves were coming in now. The first to arrive, four twelve-pounders, were brought from Black Rock by Dobbins early in April. The breezy pragmatism of the shipbuilding was less evident in the selection of the ordnance. Perry himself often left Erie to visit foundries where he supervised the casting of round shot and inspected artillery.

On the fifteenth of April two gunboats, each mounting a 32-pounder cannon, waddled off the stays into

17

John Wesley Jarvis painted this miniature oil portrait of Jesse Duncan Elliott in 1810.
THE MARINERS MUSEUM, NEWPORT NEWS, VIRGINIA

the water, and two weeks after that another gunboat was launched. Then, toward the end of May, Perry travelled up to Lake Ontario, joined Chauncey, and played a major role in the American attack on the British garrison at Fort George, at the mouth of the Niagara River. The British spiked their guns, withdrew from the fort, and decided that Fort Erie, at the other end of the river, was now also untenable. The troops were pulled out of Fort Erie, thereby making it possible for the Americans to move the small fleet that had long been stuck tight across the river at Black Rock.

There were no British guns banging away at Perry while he got the ships out of Jesse Elliott's favorite harbor, but it was still a frightful task. The vessels had to edge along the shore, towed by oxen against the strong current. All the ships made Presque Isle in safety, but the strain was beginning to tell on Perry. He was a hardy-looking type, tall and burly, but his healthy appearance was deceptive. He had not been strong as a child, and as an adult he was prey to what was then known as bilious fever. Since that convenient diagnosis was used to identify almost any intestinal disorder, it is impossible to say what his ailment really was. It is perhaps significant that it seemed to strike him after periods of prolonged stress.

In any event, Perry was sick by the time he returned to Presque Isle, and there he found most of his work force to be sick as well. Those who could work stayed at their jobs in double shifts, sawing and hammering long into the night. Sail, shot, and anchors came in from Pittsburgh, and the rest of the guns arrived.

By mid-July the job was done; the fleet was afloat in Presque Isle Bay. The two brigs, which represented about two thirds of Perry's strength—they were each a hundred and ten feet long and mounted twenty guns—were rigged and armed. Word had come through of the death of Captain James Lawrence of the frigate *Chesapeake* in his brief, luckless fight with the *Shannon*. Perry immediately named one of his brigs the *Lawrence*; the other he called the *Niagara*. Noah Brown, his work done, returned to New York. He would not be paid for his labors until March, 1814.

Perry had his fleet, but his greatest frustrations and anxieties were still ahead of him. He had no sailors to man his ships, and Chauncey, whose job it was to see that he got them, did not want to send him any. After the attack on Fort George, Chauncey had written warmly of Perry: "He was present at every point where he could be useful, under showers of musketry, but fortunately escaped unhurt." As Perry began to badger him for men, however, Chauncey soured and finally became hostile.

Yet Perry was under constant pressure to go out and fight. The Secretary of the Navy, ignorant of the situation on Lake Erie, wrote Perry demanding that he cooperate with General William Henry Harrison. After Hull had been annihilated at Detroit, Harrison raised a force that was known by the somewhat pathetic name of "the second Northwestern Army." Now Harrison had his troops in northern Ohio, facing the army of British General Henry Procter. Neither general could move without being assured of friendly control on Lake Erie; so in order to cooperate with Harrison, Perry had to secure the lake for the Americans. There was nothing that Perry wished to do more, but neither Harrison nor the Navy Department knew that he was for the moment powerless to move. The Department had been sending men to Chauncey right along. These men were designated for service on Lake Erie as well as Lake Ontario, the Department's optimistic theory being that Chauncey would wisely select the number of men needed by Perry and then dispatch them to Presque Isle. Chauncey, on the other hand, felt that he needed the men on Lake Ontario and kept them there.

Perry, by now frantic, wrote strong letters to Chauncey. He sent Dobbins out to try to drum up recruits and promised ten dollars a month to anybody who would serve for four months or until a decisive battle was fought. His recruiting drew a meager response; not more than sixty men volunteered. Then in mid-July he received an urgent order from the Navy Department and a letter from Harrison, both demanding that he sail. And on the same day the topsails of a

British fleet poked up over the horizon off Presque Isle.

In an ecstasy of frustration Perry wrote a strained, grandiloquent letter to Chauncey:

The enemy's fleet of six sail are now off the bar of this harbour. What a golden opportunity if we had men.... I am constantly looking to the eastward; every mail and every traveller from that quarter is looked to as the harbinger of the glad tidings of our men being on their way.... Give me men, sir, and I will acquire both for you and myself honour and glory on this lake, or perish in the attempt.... Think of my situation; the enemy in sight, the vessels under my command more than sufficient, and ready to make sail, and yet obliged to bite my fingers with vexation for want of men.

Perry did not worry about the British sailing in and sinking his ships; the sandbar would prevent that. But on any dark night they might land a force in boats and attack the garrison and burn his flotilla. He had some rudimentary fortifications, but they were weak and manned by a ludicrous regiment of Pennsylvania militia who, apparently afraid of the dark, would not stand watch at night. When Perry questioned their captain about this peculiar shortcoming, he received the reasonable reply "I told the boys to go, Captain, but the boys won't go."

Three days after his last letter Perry wrote Chauncey another: "For God's sake and yours, and mine, send me men and officers, and I will have them all in a day or two." But no men came, and the British fleet rode easily in the calm weather, always in view, mocking Perry's impotence.

It might have given Perry some scant solace to know that the commander of the British fleet was harassed by exactly the same difficulties that were dogging him. Robert Heriot Barclay was the sort of officer who made possible Britain's long maritime supremacy. The same age as Perry, he had spent more than half his life at sea. He had lost an arm serving with Nelson at Trafalgar, and after the great three-deckers he was used to, the scrabbly little collection of craft on Lake Erie must have seemed very modest to him. Still it represented a command, although one officer had already refused it on the grounds that the squadron was undermanned and in poor shape. Barclay reached his fleet at Amherstburg, where the Detroit River spills into the western end of Lake Erie, in the spring of 1813 and immediately went to work with the same energy Perry had shown. His first request was for men, but Yeo, who was cut from the same cloth as Chauncey, wanted to keep his sailors on Lake Ontario. Barclay complained that virtually every man Yeo did send his way was "a poor devil not worth his salt." Nevertheless Barclay managed to win the loyalty of such men as he had and worked them into an effective fighting force. It was obvious that he was in better shape than Perry when he brought his fleet out to blockade Presque Isle.

At last Chauncey doled out a few men, though they were not much to Perry's liking. "The men that came ...," Perry complained, "are a motley set, blacks, soldiers, and boys...." Chauncey sent him an exasperated reply, saying: "I regret that you are not pleased with the men sent you ... for, to my knowledge, a part of them are not surpassed by any seamen we have in the fleet; and I have yet to learn that the color of the skin, or the cut and trimmings of the coat, can affect a man's qualifications or usefulness." As it turned out, perhaps a quarter of Perry's crew were blacks, and they fought superbly when the time came.

Perry had men now—not many, but enough to sail his ships. His immediate problem was the sandbar. Though it had long protected his fleet, it was now a hindrance, for it would be a simple matter for Barclay to sweep down and shoot apart Perry's squadron while the ships were being worked across the bar into the open lake. Barclay's fleet kept watch over Perry until the end of July, and then, unaccountably, it vanished. It has been said the British captain was called away to go to a banquet across the lake; whatever the reason, his departure would prove to be a costly mistake.

Perry, rejoicing in his opponent's absence, went to work. Getting the ships out of the harbor turned out

On October 9, 1812, Elliott led a bold cutting-out expedition against two British ships moored under the guns of Fort Erie. An anonymous artist painted the coup in the 1830's.
CHICAGO HISTORICAL SOCIETY

to be a nightmarish job. Before he left, Noah Brown had built some "camels"—scows with no draft to speak of that could be flooded and then pumped out. As they were pumped dry they rose, lifting a ship braced between them enough so that she could negotiate the bar. But the bar was shallower than anyone had thought, and both the *Lawrence* and the *Niagara* got hung up on it. This meant four days of the worst kind of work: taking off all the guns and fittings, rowing them ashore, and then bringing them back again. And all the time this was going on, there was the chance that Barclay would reappear and finish things for good. He did finally reappear, but by then the *Lawrence* was out in open water, and Barclay declined to fight.

With his whole fleet across the bar Perry was joined by Jesse Duncan Elliott, who had brought down two more schooners from Buffalo, as well as two lieutenants, eight midshipmen, and eighty-nine seamen. Chauncey and Perry had long before agreed that the latter would need at least seven hundred and forty men to man his ships, but he was putting to sea with fewer than four hundred—less than a quarter of them part of the regular Navy. Nevertheless Perry was out of the harbor, with his squadron complete and ready to fight. Then, soon after his ships had cleared the bar, he wrote to the Secretary of the Navy resigning his command.

Perry must have been half mad with fatigue and strain. He was sick again, and his acrimonious exchange with Chauncey was rankling him. "I cannot serve longer," he wrote, "under an officer who has been so totally regard-

CONTINUED ON PAGE 88

OFFICE OF THE ARCHITECT OF THE CAPITOL

The small, hastily built fleet with which Perry changed our history was sketched many years after the battle by an old Lakes captain named James Van Cleve, who drew the ships above as they lay in Put-in Bay on the morning of the fight. The Niagara *is at the head of the line, followed by the flagship* Lawrence, Ariel, Caledonia, Scorpion, Somers, Tigress, *and* Porcupine, *with the tiny one-gun sloop* Trippe *bringing up the rear. At left, Perry leaves his gutted flagship in order to bring up the rest of his fleet. The state of Ohio commissioned this painting from William Henry Powell in 1873; it now hangs in the Senate wing of the Capitol. After the battle British and American officers were given a common burial. Louis Chevalier painted the moody scene of the service, below, in 1825.*

By DAVID DAVIDSON

The Story of the Century

On the raw, gusty night of March 1, 1932, in the Sourland Hills of New Jersey, the twenty-month-old son of Charles A. Lindbergh and the former Anne Morrow, their first-born, was kidnapped from his nursery. Discarded nearby was a rough-made sectional ladder with a broken lower rung. A ransom note, with expressions and misspellings that suggested a writer whose first language was German, was left in the nursery. It led, on the night of April 2 in a Bronx cemetery, to the payment of fifty thousand dollars by an intermediary to a lone extortioner. But the child was not returned. Various hoaxers entered the picture, and underworld emissaries sought vainly to make contact with any gangsters who might have been involved.

On May 12 truckers stopping in woods not far from the Lindbergh home came across the child's body.

Meanwhile a number of the ransom bills, of which police had recorded the serial numbers, began to appear in the New York area. A large part of the ransom, incidentally, had been paid in gold notes, which bore a yellow seal on the face and were redeemable by the Treasury in gold specie. By a decree of the Roosevelt administration taking the country off the gold standard in 1933, gold currency was officially withdrawn from circulation. Such ransom bills therefore became all the more conspicuous.

On September 15, 1934, some two and a half years after the kidnapping, a New York gas-station attendant jotted down the license number of a driver who not only paid with a $10 gold note but boasted of having a "hundred more" at home. Four days later, after trailing the car owner about, FBI agents and New York police arrested him—a German-born carpenter named Bruno Richard Hauptmann, who lived in the north Bronx with his wife and infant son. In his wallet they found a $20 ransom bill, and $14,600 more in the garage behind his rented home.

Hauptmann went on trial for murder in the Hunterdon County Court at Flemington, a little town in the rolling farmland of west New Jersey, on January 2, 1935. "We realized," said Lindbergh, testifying at the trial, "that after this circumstance had originally happened the sequence of events would probably be peculiar, not according to the ordinary logic of life."

In fact, the tragic kidnap-murder of the Lindbergh baby became the occasion of a long-running carnival-circus that took one bizarre turn after another and ultimately reached its low, in many respects, with the trial of Hauptmann.

Outside the whitewashed native-stone courthouse in Flemington, a marketplace for chicken and egg farmers some seventy miles southwest of New York City, where nothing much had ever happened before in two centuries, souvenir peddlers promptly swarmed in to hawk tiny wooden replicas of the kidnap ladder.

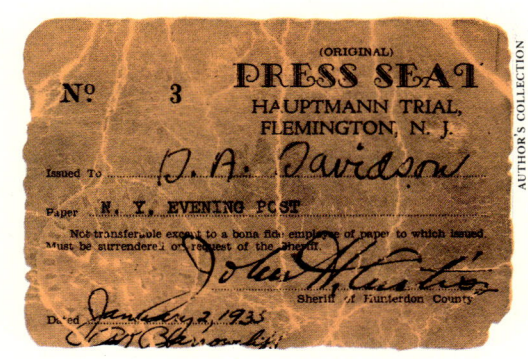

On the first Sunday of the trial, when the courthouse was opened to sightseers, an estimated sixty thousand visitors from as far away as Chicago and Washington, according to their entries in the "guest book" the local sheriff provided, descended on Flemington, whose normal population was less than three thousand. Some twenty thousand automobiles, at times moving only three miles an hour and at other times not at all, choked the roads all the way back to New York and Philadelphia.

At the courthouse deputy sheriffs served as barkers, pointing out the main attractions. Tourists elbowed one another for the thrill of sitting in the chair Lindbergh occupied daily as an observer, marked with a sheet of paper

Above, right: The special press card issued to the author for the Lindbergh kidnapping trial. Left: Cheerfully posing in a snowstorm outside the courthouse, spectators carry tiny replicas of the kidnap ladder that were sold by souvenir peddlers.

23

breezily inscribed "Lindy." But they backed off with a shudder from the camp chair assigned to Hauptmann; only three brave sightseers risked it all day. Hundreds had themselves photographed in the judge's place and carved their initials into the bench. The century-old witness chair had to be nailed down lest it be carried off.

As the trial progressed attendance became an absolute must for the café-society set presided over by that huge, pear-shaped, rumpled arbiter of elegance Elsa Maxwell. Packs of "women in mink," as they came to be called, became a regular feature of the court sessions, along with Broadway and Hollywood stars such as Lynne Fontanne, Clifton Webb, Jack Benny, and Estelle Taylor. The Union Hotel, the town's only hostelry, which normally served fifty meals a day, dished out a thousand for the duration of the trial, and—significantly—two thousand drinks a day.

An inside group of newspapermen, doing their best to live up to the lifestyle of Ben Hecht and Charles MacArthur's rowdy play *The Front Page*, concocted a special trial anthem, adapted from the German beer-garden ditty "Schnitzelbank," that ridiculed almost everybody and everything connected with the trial. A printable sample stanza went:

Ist das nicht der noon recess?
Ya, das ist der noon recess.
Schmells der court like Bronx Express?
Ya, like rush-hour Bronx Express.

During the six weeks of the trial some dozens of volunteer "confessions" were received from all over the country, "clearing" Hauptmann. The confessors turned out to be a variety of publicity seekers, psychopaths, and convicts hoping to wangle a brief vacation from their prison cells by being brought to Flemington to testify.

Nevertheless, for all this nightmarish hullabaloo, Justice Thomas W. Trenchard, a massive man who looked like a monument of Jurisprudence, managed miraculously to keep a firm hand on the trial proceedings and to guide them so fairly and dignifiedly and humanely (he bought rubbers for the entire jury to wade through the winter slush on their way to and from the courthouse) that no error was ever laid against him during the many appeals before Hauptmann died in the electric chair at the New Jersey State Prison in Trenton on April 3, 1936.

Why this mass hysteria that for six weeks made Flemington a world news center? The main reason, of course, was that Lindbergh, the Lone Eagle, was still a world hero seven years after his epic solo flight across the Atlantic. Also this was a time when sensational murder trials, including the Hall-Mills and Snyder-Gray cases of a few years before, were the favorite reading matter of the newspaper public.

Reporters came from every continent to pour out as much as a million words a day from the little courthouse on a web of 168 specially installed lines that included direct wires to London, Paris, Berlin, and Sydney. It was the largest setup ever created for a news event, including the World Series and Olympic games. Technicians estimated that for the duration of the trial Flemington had a communications system large enough to provide normal service for a city of a million.

Newspapermen enjoyed calling the Hauptmann trial "the Story of the Century," airily by-passing World War I. It was nevertheless a fact that day after day on the front pages of America, and many foreign journals as well, the trial was given top play over such simultaneous, and ultimately more significant, events as the first of the Moscow trials of Old Bolsheviks; the first appeasement of Adolf Hitler, this by the return to Germany of the Saarland territory (after which New Jersey's local Sourland was misnamed); and the Roosevelt administration's introduction of a key piece of New Deal legislation, the Social Security Act.

Seating capacity of the courtroom, with its church-pew spectator benches and some extra facilities, was no more than five hundred, and there was a daily struggle for admission that went all the way from primitive elbowing to ruses like obtaining pretend witness subpoenas from friendly lawyers in the case. I happened to be one of a hundred and fifty privileged newspapermen who were issued special press passes. My own blood-red ticket, imprinted in black, entitled me to Press Seat No. 3, which consisted of about twenty meager inches of sitting space in the first of two rows of unpainted pine benches and tables that were installed directly behind the enclosure for judge, defendant, lawyers, and witnesses.

There, in my narrow lebensraum, wearing down ten pencils daily, I contributed some five thousand words a day of the running story for the New York *Post*. This was a consecutive, chronological account of all that happened in the courtroom while it was happening: question-and-answer testimony, an evaluation of the same in relation to previous testimony and happenings, description of the appearance and behavior of the witnesses, skirmishes of the lawyers, reaction of the defendant and spectators. And every word of it had to be written by hand on manuscript-size sheets, passed up the aisle by messengers, and relayed to the attic, where a telegrapher especially assigned to me transmitted my running account to the *Post*, an evening paper, where it would be set up in type and printed only minutes later.

Simultaneously my senior partner, James Martindale, would be writing leads to the story, including revisions and bulletins, that would go at the top of the chronological account, changing as new developments occurred.

The telegraphers on such assignments had a knack for learning quickly to decipher the scrawls of their reporter wards. Though I had regularly flunked penmanship all through elementary school, my own personal guardian, Joe, of Postal Telegraph (I never learned the rest of his name), failed only once in interpreting my six-week output of 150,000 words. On the fourth day of the trial, during testimony involving the kidnap ladder, a sheet of my copy came rustling back in reverse action over the chain of transmission from the attic. A marginal note from Joe inquired as to whether a certain circled hieroglyphic was to be read as "nail hole" or "mastermind," indicating the broad spectrum of my indecipherability. (It was "nail hole.")

A newcomer to the *Post*, I was the

youngest member of a staff of ten that our legendary city editor, the late Walter Lister, selected to take with him to Flemington. A brilliant newspaperman and an incidental playwright who coauthored one of America's first expressionist plays, *Spread Eagle,* Lister was a severe taskmaster. At the time he was earnestly trying to model himself on that great archetype of the sadistic city editor, Charles Chapin of the old New York *World,* who not only tormented his staff fiendishly but murdered his wife and wound up editing the Sing Sing Prison house organ. Lister fell short of uxoricide but, as next best, created legend by firing his favorite drinking companion, whose wife was very pregnant, one blizzardy Christmas Eve.

How I came to be tapped for the assignment was that, first, I had developed a knack of writing fast and could compose up to sixty words a minute of a news story under deadline, a valued skill on evening newspapers, where edition after edition is chasing the news as it is happening.

Further, in a series of flukes my life had become oddly linked to Hauptmann's from the day of his arrest to the day of his execution. Again and again I was consistently lucky on the Hauptmann story as on no other story before or after.

For instance, on the day of his arrest I was sent to get an interview with Hauptmann's wife, Anna, at the friend's apartment where she had taken shelter with her infant son. I arrived to find I had been preceded by some two dozen reporters who had exhausted every possible dodge to get Mrs. Hauptmann to open the apartment door and submit to an interview. They had posed as telegraph messengers, lawyers, delivery boys, even po-

At the trial (from top to bottom): Mrs. Anne Morrow Lindbergh arrives, escorted by Assistant Attorney General Robert Peacock. As guards look on, the accused, Bruno Richard Hauptmann, talks to his wife, Anna. Charles A. Lindbergh took the witness stand on January 3, 1935, to testify about the kidnapping of his twenty-month-old son. Some newspapermen had to work by candlelight when a courthouse fuse blew.

licemen. They had climbed a rickety back-alley fire escape and banged on the shaded and locked windows in vain. One had even yelled "Fire!" Among the crestfallen crowd were A. J. Liebling, Dorothy Kilgallen, and Joseph Mitchell, all of later fame.

Within sixty seconds of my arrival on the scene I became the only reporter Mrs. Hauptmann admitted, on that day and for two weeks thereafter (until a Hearst paper, the New York *Journal,* bought her away from me with money and put her on their payroll as an exclusive property). What did the trick for me was a completely fortuitous decision the year before, while I was working in Baltimore, to fill out the long provincial evenings by taking a six-month Berlitz course in German.

Now I had but to shout through the door of Mrs. Hauptmann's hide-out in German: "Journalist. Wish to interview you about your husband's innocence!" At once the door opened, and Mrs. Hauptmann asked, in German: "Who spoke German?" I stepped forward, and she let me in.

It was the most taxing interview I held in ten years as a newspaperman. Though I could understand Mrs. Hauptmann well enough, my own spoken German began to flag. But Mrs. Hauptmann soon began to accept questions from me in English; more serious was the fact that whenever I reached for my pencil and wad of copy paper to take notes, Mrs. Hauptmann froze in her tracks. So I put away pencil and paper altogether and as best I could committed the entire two-hour interview to memory.

Among the things she told me was that her Richard could not possibly have kidnapped and killed a child, because he was much too gentle and concerned about all living things. Once, she said, he had nearly wrecked their car to avoid hitting a squirrel. Often he had scolded people who picked flowers in the park instead of letting them live for all the public to enjoy.

A plain, stocky woman who looked exactly like what she had been before her marriage, a hardworking waitress in a bakery-restaurant, she was yet able to evoke a touching, even romantic, moment in her life with Hauptmann. A few months after they had met, in German circles in the Bronx, she said, he took her to a park bench for a talk. There, she said, he asked her to marry him but said that there was something he had to tell her before she gave her answer—that he was in the United States illegally. Because of some "trouble" as a youth in Germany he had been unable to obtain a visa but had smuggled himself into the United States as a stowaway on a ship. She had taken his hand in hers, she said, and kissed him and joined her life to his.

The same day as that first interview with Mrs. Hauptmann, I went to the little garage behind their home and poked through the mounds of debris left by FBI men who had torn the interior apart in finding the $14,600 of ransom bills. For no reason except the mild irony involved I picked up and took away with me a German detective novel entitled *Die Finanzen des Grossherzogs* ("The Finances of the Grand Duke"). At the time I had no reason to pay particular attention to the name inscribed on the flyleaf, Isidor Fisch.

Within twenty-four hours it developed that Hauptmann was trying to clear himself by pinning the ransom money on an acquaintance now dead with whom he had had some minor dealings in fur skins—Isidor Fisch. I learned also that all the police agencies involved were hunting desperately for a sample of Fisch's handwriting to compare with that of the kidnapper's notes. The *Post,* after printing a facsimile and analysis of the Fisch signature from *Die Finanzen des Grossherzogs,* was glad to accommodate the police.

So it went for me even during the trial. One day, as Hauptmann was being taken under guard from the courtroom during a recess and passing the kidnap ladder, which was standing against the wall in evidence, I lunged toward him impulsively and obtained a "world exclusive," a first interview of two succinct sentences:

Q. Bruno, did you make that ladder?
A. I would be a second-hand carpenter if I make such a ladder.

I was struck by the incongruously high-pitched voice that came out of that virile athletic body, but I was later to observe a similar phenomenon in such undoubted manly specimens as Jack Dempsey, Fiorello La Guardia, Ernest Hemingway, and General Patton.

A definite obstacle to the proceedings were the mink-clad ladies from café society (the generational parent of the jet set and grandparent of the Beautiful People) who swarmed to the trial like the knitting women at the base of the guillotine during the Terror. Throughout the sessions they chatted, tittered, and giggled without concern for the fact that a man charged with the murder of a baby was on trial for his life. So many of them turned up in Flemington that the *Journal* assigned one of its society columnists, a Mrs. Sigourney Thayer who wrote under the house pseudonym "Madame Flutterby," to spend full time at the trial reporting nothing but the activities of the women in mink.

In an angry piece for the *New York Times* novelist Edna Ferber wrote: "I found all the Maxwell party countersigns and passwords were being cooed back and forth. All the mink coats were saying to the Savile Row topcoats and burgundy mufflers, 'Hello, darling! How are you? Isn't this divine?'"

But high as Miss Ferber soared in her indignation, I believe she fell short of the social commentary we put together in the *Post* by simply quoting from the *Encyclopedia Britannica*'s wholly objective description of the mink as a "fur-bearing animal... of the weasel family... Few mammals are as voracious and bloodthirsty. ... The female is of a savage disposition."

Miss Ferber was herself one of another genus, the "trained seal," as we working reporters called them, celebrities in other writing media who were sent to the trial by various newspapers and news agencies to catch a quick impression and make profound observations. Also present were Alexander Woollcott, the sage of the *New Yorker*, and novelists Fannie Hurst, Kathleen Norris, and Ford Madox Ford, who invariably found themselves thoroughly confused by the twists and turns of the testimony and would eventually appeal to some fifty-dollar-a-week reporter of the working press to guide them through the maze.

As an aspiring young novelist I was flattered to do service for the most distinguished trained seal of the lot, Ford Madox Ford, a huge, kindly mass of a man well described at the time as resembling a beached whale and very near destitution because of the meager sales of his novels in the Depression. At Ford's request I showed him around town so he could stock up on overnight supplies. At the drugstore he asked, wistfully, for "the very smallest quantity of toothpaste that you sell" (a ten-cent tube) and elsewhere for "the cheapest spirits you stock, and the very smallest quantity" (this last was a half pint of applejack, the highly potent and potable *vin du pays* of Hunterdon County, priced at seventy-five cents).

Though the strongest aspects of the case against Hauptmann proved to be a mass of solid, objective evidence of a kind that laymen mistakenly downgrade because it is "circumstantial," there were also a host of eyewitnesses who claimed to have beheld Hauptmann in a variety of damaging situations. Chief among them was John F. Condon ("Jafsie," as he called himself), a heavyset, seventy-four-year-old retired elementary-school teacher from "the beautiful borough of the Bronx." In one of the more bizarre turns of the case he became the intermediary in the ransom negotiations simply by writing a letter to a neighborhood newspaper offering his services —with the astonishing result that the kidnapper, whom he later positively identified as Hauptmann, got in touch with him at once and met with him twice face to face.

Other eyewitnesses proved far less convincing, including an eighty-seven-year-old veteran of the Franco-Prus-

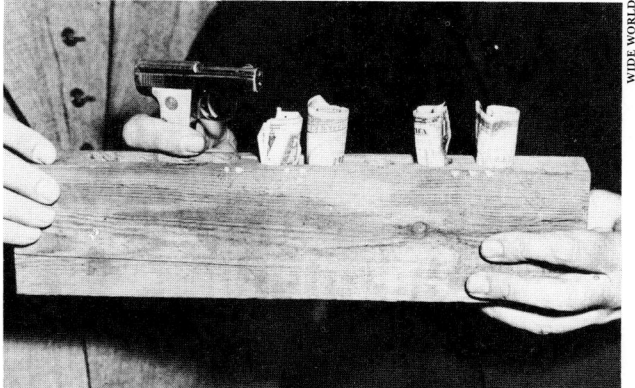

The evidence (from top to bottom): Police rip apart the roof of Hauptmann's garage in search of the ransom. Clerks carry the kidnap ladder, minus its lower rung, into the trial. Photographers put currency into the plank found in the garage to show how some of the ransom bills were hidden; the gun was in the gouged-out section to the left. Chief Prosecutor David Wilentz displays specimens of Hauptmann's writing.

sian War, Amandus Hochmuth, who claimed to have seen Hauptmann clearly at a distance of twenty-five feet as Hauptmann's car whipped around a bend in the road toward the Lindbergh place. Even at that distance, said Hochmuth, he could see Hauptmann flush.

To test the fundamental reliability of eyewitness testimony, a fellow reporter on the *Post*, the late Henry Paynter, devised an impish experiment in which I had the pleasure of accompanying him one weekend. Equipped with a batch of photos of nine nationally prominent persons, we went on a tour among the farmer neighbors of the Lindberghs in the Sourland Hills. In each case we showed the photos and asked whether any such persons had been seen in the neighborhood at the time of the kidnapping. The responses were fairly astonishing. For instance, a photo of General Hugh S. Johnson, former chief of Roosevelt's National Recovery Administration, brought the following comments:

"I remember him all right. He was coming up the road dressed like a tramp."

"Isn't he that Whately fellow, the English butler of the Lindberghs?"

"That's a tough face. That's one I'll never forget. If ever I see that colt a-foolin' around my traps, I'd sure as hell go for my rifle."

Concerning the notably mild-mannered Dr. Rexford Guy Tugwell, New Deal economist and Assistant Secretary of Agriculture, one witness remarked: "He has a criminal face. Isn't that the Mr. Schmidt who killed himself around here?"

Justice Joseph Force Crater of New York, who disappeared in 1930 and has never been traced to this day, evoked these comments:

"He was around. He said he was a newspaper fellow."

"Oh yes, he was prowling around here with that other fellow [Dr. Tugwell], asking the way to the Lindbergh place."

Looking at the photo of Mayor La Guardia of New York, one of our witnesses declared: "I saw him driving in a blue sedan with something, maybe a ladder."

Not one of the persons questioned identified the photo of America's Public Enemy No. 1 of the time, Al Capone.

Another aspect of the eyewitness business developed when Hauptmann's chief counsel, Edward J. Reilly—a florid, carnation-wearing old-time criminal lawyer known as the "Bull of Brooklyn"—began presenting the case for the defense. He led off with a string of Good Samaritans who had come forward to volunteer a variety of testimony intended to provide Hauptmann with alibis on critical dates and implicate other figures instead. Of a batch of seven such witnesses each was destroyed before he left the stand. It was proved on cross-examination that five had prison records and one had had three stays in mental hospitals. As for the seventh, an actor-taxi driver, he broke into a string of Will Rogers impersonations that made it hard to take him seriously.

The prosecution was able to confound these defense witnesses quickly through an elaborate checking procedure. The moment the witnesses gave name and address, special squads of New Jersey and New York police went to work checking local, FBI, and other files by telephone. The next day five more scheduled defense witnesses failed to show, and five more the day after.

Reilly, whose ornate dress (morning coat and striped pants, along with the daily carnation) did not go down well in backwoods Flemington, was not devoid of a sense of humor. In the last week of the trial, sitting next to his table at lunch in the Union Hotel, I heard him make a totally uninhibited comment on the nature and quality of his own witnesses. Addressing yet another would-be volunteer who had come to his table, Reilly bellowed: "You've never been convicted of a crime? You've never been in a lunatic asylum? I can't use you as a witness."

The city-slicker versus local-yokel antagonisms, heightened by Reilly's big-town elegance, went right down the line, with victory not always going to the New Yorkers. Somehow the country boys managed again and again to clean out the visitors in impromptu crap games, including among their victims, on one occasion, that quintessence of Broadway sophistication Damon Runyon, who did a daily trial story for the Hearst syndicate.

And there was the dark night when two of my *Post* colleagues fell for the most elementary rube racket of country carnivals. Coming back along Main Street to our rented quarters in the home of a local dentist, they were carrying a surprise treat of a case of beer and two dozen hamburgers when they were accosted by two Flemington youths who taunted them with obscenities. Carefully putting beer and hamburgers down on the sidewalk, my colleagues gave chase to their two tormentors. Promptly a third and a fourth yokel came out of the shadows and made off with our midnight snack.

Most causes célèbres seem to have a revisionist aftermath in which theories are offered to turn the official verdict upside down. The Hauptmann trial is no exception. To this day, forty-one years later, whenever it comes out at a social gathering that I covered his trial, the first question I am inevitably asked is "Did Hauptmann really do it?"

My instant answer echoes the closing argument of the chief prosecutor, Attorney General David Wilentz of New Jersey, that naturally no movie camera was present in the nursery to make a record of the break-in, but that a mass of other evidence, beyond the eyewitness testimony, leads to Hauptmann and nobody else.

1. Hauptmann was found in possession of a large number of ransom bills.

2. A full year before Hauptmann was arrested, a federal lumber expert, Arthur Koehler of Wisconsin, by a patient and brilliant process involving forty thousand mills and suppliers, had traced the ponderosa pine of the kidnap ladder to a lumberyard near Hauptmann's home where he bought his own supplies and often put in a few days' work. Koehler was actually visiting the yard one day while Hauptmann was there.

3. One rail in the ladder was proved to have been ripped from the flooring in Hauptmann's attic, apparently when he ran short of lumber to finish the ladder. The positioning and angle of

nail holes in the rail matched exactly the holes left in the joist from which the plank had been torn.

4. Inside a closet, on a wall, in Hauptmann's home had been jotted down the telephone number John Condon had given the kidnapper during the ransom negotiations.

5. Work sheets in the construction of the high-rise Majestic Apartments on Central Park West, in New York, where Hauptmann was employed early in 1932, show that he went to work neither on the day of the kidnapping nor on that of the passing of the ransom.

6. After the date of the ransom payment Hauptmann never again worked at his trade, or at any, but spent much of his time—and money—playing the stock market. Not successfully.

The one question that remains open to this day is whether Hauptmann had an accomplice, and this opens up the subsidiary question of whether he deliberately murdered the baby after taking it from the nursery, or whether the child was killed in an accidental fall when a rung of the ladder broke.

If death was accidental, then Hauptmann would have required an accomplice to harbor the child while Hauptmann was meeting Lindbergh's intermediary. If death was deliberate, no accomplice was necessary. At any rate, the FBI very early cleared Mrs. Hauptmann of any connection with the case. And FBI accountants produced their own kind of proof that Hauptmann was a loner in that they traced to him—either by his expenditures or cash left in hand or stock account balances—almost the entire fifty thousand dollars of the ransom.

Then, too, beyond all this, there was a conversation I overheard one day during a recess between two local

CONTINUED ON PAGE 93

The carnival atmosphere (from top to bottom): Hauptmann's dapper chief counsel, Edward J. Reilly, shakes hands with a young fan. A Flemington restaurant offers a ghoulish bill of fare. The author is seated at far right in a privileged spot, usually reserved for staff, at the popular bar of the Union Hotel. A typical scene outside the courthouse shows newsreel cameramen atop cars waiting to film celebrities at the trial.

Johns Hopkins

HOW A FARSIGHTED QUAKER MERCHANT AND FOUR GREAT DOCTORS BROUGHT FORTH, WITH MADDENING SLOWNESS, ONE OF THE FINEST MEDICAL CENTERS IN THE WORLD

By CAROLINE JONES FRANZ

In 1884, after he was offered an appointment to the medical faculty of the newly created Johns Hopkins University, Dr. William Henry Welch wrote to his stepmother: "Such great things are expected of the medical faculty at the Johns Hopkins in the way of achievement and of reform of medical education in this country that I feel oppressed by the weight of responsibility. A reputation there will not be so cheaply earned as at Bellevue, but in so far the stimulus to do good work will be the greater. I shall be surrounded by cultivated, refined and distinguished men, who will estimate a man for his intrinsic worth and not for money or glitter."

Welch's concern over the potential responsibility was not exaggerated. The first physician to receive such an appointment to the fledgling university, he was going against the advice of practically all of his friends, relatives, and colleagues. With such great hospitals as Bellevue in New York beckoning, why would any self-respecting professor of pathology decide to remove himself to the backwater of Baltimore, forsaking the allure and prestige of a ready-made career? As Welch reasoned it: "It is a mistake to believe that a reputation made there [at Hopkins] would not equal one made in New York in my line of work. In practice of medicine of course it would not, but the results of research and discovery redound equally to one's reputation whether made in Oshkosh or in New York." And so he accepted.

Although the undergraduate part of the university had opened on a limited basis by October of 1876, nothing was finished by the time Welch received his offer—more than a decade after the death of the school's benefactor, a wealthy merchant who had died late in 1873. Hopkins, a lifelong bachelor, had genuine philanthropic interests but had trouble deciding what to do with his fortune. As the son of a prosperous Quaker tobacco farmer from Anne Arundel County, Maryland, Hopkins had enjoyed a pampered and leisurely childhood, though he was one of a brood of eleven children. But the hard realities of the working life abruptly dropped onto his young shoulders when, in 1807, his father's adherence to a new Quaker policy led him to free all his slaves. Suddenly young Johns— it was a family name—was forced to drop out of school at age twelve and go to work in the fields.

Finding the life of a farmer not to his liking, Hopkins waited until he was seventeen and then went to work for his uncle Gerard Hopkins, a wholesale grocer in Baltimore. He soon proved his ability as a shrewd merchant, capably handling the shop whenever his uncle went away on

A more diverse group than the founding doctors in John Singer Sargent's portrait could scarcely be imagined. They are, from left to right: William H. Welch, who took the job against all advice; William Osler, a practical joker; W. S. Halsted, who fought a grueling battle with drugs; Howard Kelly, an ardent Bible-thumper. Above is Hopkins himself, about 1870.
BOTH: THE JOHNS HOPKINS UNIVERSITY ARCHIVES

31

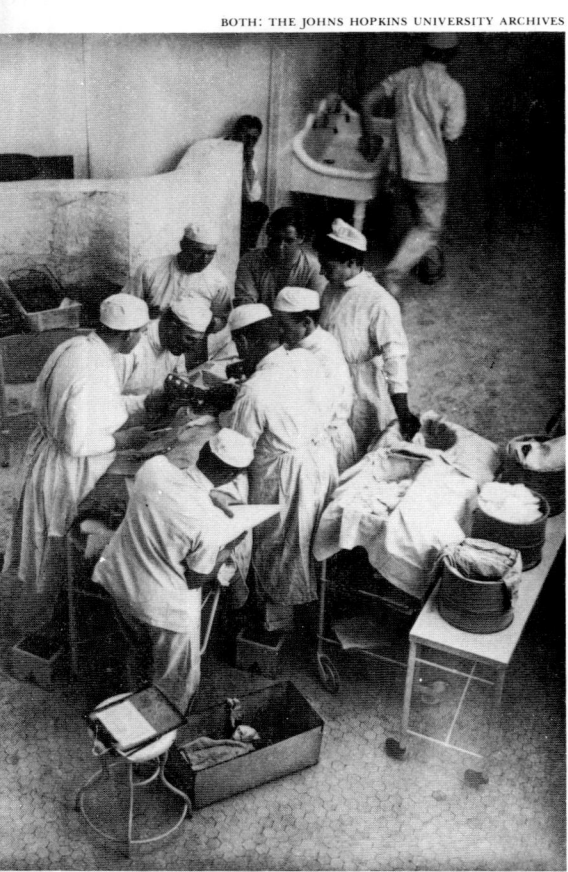

Surrounded by young doctors, Halsted performs one of his careful operations in the school's surgical amphitheater in 1904.

business and making excellent suggestions for improving sales. But when Johns announced a few years later that he wished to marry his first cousin Elizabeth, Gerard Hopkins' only daughter, the friendly working relationship came to an abrupt end, for his aunt and uncle were appalled at the "incestuous" suggestion. So, having saved sufficient capital to set himself up, and with a little help from his family, he went into business alone as a supplier of whiskey, tobacco, and other staples. He quickly prospered, making $200,000 worth of sales in the first year. But he never courted another woman.

Within a few years Hopkins had branched out, selling provisions as far south as North Carolina and as far west as Ohio. By 1847 his now-established wealth and keen business sense had created quite a reputation for him, and he was named, in that year, president of the Merchants' National Bank of Baltimore and a director of the rapidly expanding Baltimore & Ohio Railroad. The B&O was a further boost to his flourishing fortune; by the time he died, he owned fifteen thousand shares of its stock. During the Civil War he was one of three bankers who loaned the city of Baltimore $500,000; later, during the Panic of 1873, he advanced $900,000 to the railroad to help it meet its interest payments.

With increasing age Hopkins began to ponder more and more the problem of disposing of his considerable fortune "for the good of humanity." There were plenty of advisers, and someone eventually pointed out that it would be unique for Hopkins to bestow his name on both a university *and* a hospital. A charter was obtained in 1867 and a board of trustees appointed. Hopkins set down his stipulations for the Johns Hopkins University and Hospital: of his estimated estate of $7,000,000 half was to go toward the university, of which the school of medicine would be a part, and half to the hospital. The capital was to be totally invested in either stocks or real estate, with interest paying the cost of construction. It was a unique arrangement; it would be the first hospital subject to the authority of a university, with the medical school tagging along after both. Eventually the hospital and the university would have separate boards of trustees.

Hopkins had an elaborate conception of what his hospital would be. In March, 1873, he set down his vision in a letter to the twelve trustees:

It is my wish that the plan thus chosen shall be one which will permit symmetrical additions to the buildings which will be first constructed, in order that you may ultimately be able to receive four hundred patients; and that it shall provide for a Hospital, which shall, in construction and arrangement, compare favorably with any other institution of like character in this country or in Europe.... The indigent sick of this city and its environs, without regard to sex, age, or color, who may require surgical or medical treatment, and who can be received into the Hospital without peril to the other inmates, and the poor of this city and State, of all races, who are stricken down by any casualty, shall be received into the Hospital, without charge, for such periods of time and under such regulations as you may prescribe.... It will be your special duty to secure for the service of the Hospital surgeons and physicians of the highest character and greatest skill.... I wish the large grounds surrounding the Hospital buildings ... to be so laid out and planted with trees and flowers as to afford solace to the sick and be an ornament to the section of the city in which the grounds are located.... In all your arrangements in relation to this Hospital, you will bear constantly in mind that it is my wish and purpose that the institution shall ultimately form a part of the Medical School of that University for which I have made ample provision by my will.

He died of pneumonia nine months later at the age of seventy-eight, never to see the ground broken.

It was two years before the trustees sent out invitations to several well-known authorities on hospital planning, asking them to come up with ideas for the construction of the hospital. The job eventually went to John Shaw Billings, a veteran army doctor and sanitation expert whose concept was the pavilion arrangement: a main building with separate wards branching out from it. Billings was named medical adviser to the hospital, and construction began in 1877 on a thirteen-acre lot that was previously the site of the Maryland Hospital for the Insane. Because the principal of the bequest was not to be invaded, however, and annual interest was only $125,000, it was twelve years before the hospital was completed.

In June of 1883 the trustees told Billings, in his role as medical consultant, to set about the business of selecting the staff of the hospital and future medical school. He had once met William Welch in Germany and been quite impressed with the young pathologist. It was Billings' recommendation to the president of the new university, Daniel C. Gilman, that he offer the first professorship, that of pathology, to Welch, thus luring him away from Bellevue in New York.

Welch was the son, grandson, and nephew of country doctors in Norfolk, Connecticut. Entering Yale at the age of sixteen, he had been a brilliant student—but in the classics. In fact, he had always had an aversion to things medical as a youth, saying he couldn't "bear the sight of blood and the sight and sound of pain." He wanted to teach the classics at Yale, but the coveted position went to a friend. So after a bit of fatherly pressure he entered Columbia University's College of Physicians and Surgeons in 1872, graduating in 1875. (The standard medical-school curriculum at that time was three years, with no admissions requirements, no grades, and only one final examination.) Wisely assessing the profession and its practitioners in the United States, Welch realized that the best clinical research was going on in Europe, especially Germany and Austria, and knew that he could perfect his craft only by going there to study. He spent the best part of the next two years abroad, working under some of the foremost medical scholars of the age. He returned to New York in 1878 and remained there working in his laboratory at Bellevue and doing part-time teaching until he received the summons from Gilman in 1883. He did manage to squeeze in one more year in Germany before finally delivering himself to Hopkins, and thus was well founded in the latest techniques and theories of bacteriology and pathology. He was especially impressed with John Shaw Billings' assurance that the laboratories under construction were to be on the German model and that the medical school, when completed, would have high admission standards.

"I begin with a salary of $4,000—the others [university professors, not medical faculty] mostly began with $3,000—I am the eighth full professor yet appointed in the history of the university," he wrote his father. "I am to have all of the paid associates and assistants I need, so that I can be the head and not the hands for everything. I do not have to pay the running expenses of the laboratory. I can develop my field in Baltimore unhampered by traditions. The surroundings are scholarly and academic, and of a much higher order than those of Bellevue College in my opinion." According to Simon and James Thomas Flexner, Welch's biographers,

"The New York medical profession was aghast; in all the annals of American medicine there had been no instance of so ambitious and able a young man exchanging a brilliant future in practice for an academic professorship in which the rewards were to be like the rewards of a German professor, with the difference of less opportunity for independent work and less remuneration." Apparently some medical friends gave Welch a going-away party, sending him off with this comforting thought: "You may become a connoisseur of terrapin and madeira, but as a pathologist, good-bye."

As a promising young doctor and thus highly eligible bachelor, Welch was keenly pursued by Baltimore hostesses. But since he was a short, portly, plain-looking man not given to frivolous conversation, the young ladies were disappointed. Nonetheless, as a genial and well-read companion he continued to be invited to dinner parties. "I accepted five dinner invitations in succession," he told his sister, "some being very handsome affairs. I attended recently a beautiful reception at the Bonapartes. This is rather more gayety than I care for." Like his hospital's benefactor he remained a bachelor for the rest of his life.

It became part of Welch's responsibility to help Billings recruit more qualified physicians for the new staff, first for the hospital and subsequently as teachers for the medical school. One man who stuck in his mind was William S. Halsted, a superb young surgeon whom he had met in New York in 1878.

Halsted had also graduated from Yale and the College of Physicians and Surgeons, two years behind Welch, and spent two years of intensive postgraduate study abroad. A member of the staffs of several hospitals in New

CONTINUED ON PAGE 98

On a pleasant day at the turn of the century, convalescent patients sun themselves on a bridge between the administration annex at the left and the main administration building.

33

Daniel Morgan, in immaculate buckskins, stands with his comrades in this detail from John Trumbull's painting of Burgoyne's surrender.
YALE UNIVERSITY ART GALLERY

XVI Men of the Revolution

By RICHARD M. KETCHUM

A few months after the shooting began, the besiegers and the beleaguered of Boston became aware of a new presence on the scene. It was a new man, so to speak, with a new weapon; and since there were some fourteen hundred of them—boisterous, cocksure frontiersmen, clothed in fringed buckskin shirts and leggings, given at the slightest encouragement to demonstrating their skill with their deadly-accurate long rifles—it was difficult for anyone in the vicinity of Cambridge, Massachusetts, to ignore them. To the delight and amazement of onlookers, they could put one ball after another into a seven-inch target at 250 yards, and to the dismay of George Washington, who was trying to fashion an army capable of standing up to the British, the backwoodsmen proved as unrestrained a lot of ruffians as could be imagined, hopelessly unsuited to discipline.

In June the Continental Congress had resolved to enlist ten companies of riflemen—men known, as Richard Henry Lee put it, for their "amazing hardihood." As may be supposed, no ordinary mortal was capable of commanding the respect and loyalty of these independent, unpredictable characters, and it fell to the likes of Daniel Morgan to do so. Born in New Jersey about 1735, Morgan had run away from home at the age of seventeen and grew up on the wilderness edge of Pennsylvania and western Virginia. He became a teamster, hauling freight between remote frontier settlements, and in 1755 was hired as a wagoner for the Braddock expedition against Fort Duquesne. No teamster had any use for authority, and Morgan was no exception; when he was reprimanded by a British officer on the march, he knocked the man down. For his trouble he was sentenced to five hundred lashes, and in later years Morgan—who was scarred for life—liked to say that he owed the British one stripe because the fellow who flogged him had miscounted.

Three years later he was an ensign with the Virginia militia, carrying dispatches, when an Indian bullet went through his neck, taking all the teeth on one side of his mouth with it. He married and settled down to farming in the Shenandoah Valley, but only temporarily; in 1763 he served as a lieutenant in Pontiac's War, and in 1774 he was fighting Indians again in the Ohio Valley.

Over six feet tall, he had a superb physique and a notoriously short temper. He could barely read or write, but that was no great handicap on the frontier; Morgan possessed a fine mind, an abundance of common sense, and the acute perceptions of a man who had learned to survive hardship and continuous danger.

After the Revolution began, we catch our first glimpse of him in mid-summer of 1775, riding into Cambridge at the head of the company he had raised in Virginia and brought north at a pace of over twenty-eight miles a day. Next we find him in the van of Benedict Arnold's march to Quebec (with his ever-resourceful riflemen stealing flour from other units when their own food ran out), enduring that incredible ordeal that was one of the true epics of American military history. In the disastrous assault on Quebec, Morgan took command when Arnold was wounded and led his detachment against a barricade in the narrow streets of the Lower Town. As his head appeared over the barrier a musket volley knocked him backward; one bullet went through his cap, another singed his beard, and powder burned his face. On his feet again, he vaulted over the top of the fence, roaring at his men to follow, calling on the enemy to surrender. But time was against him. While he waited for reinforcements more British and Canadians filtered into position, surrounding his command, and at the last Morgan stood with his back against the wall of a house, facing his enemies with drawn sword, tears of rage and frustration streaming down his cheeks. His men begged him not to sacrifice his life, and the Virginian, seeing a priest in the crowd, handed his sword to him rather than yield it to a British officer.

A captive until late in 1776, Morgan rejoined Washington's army in April of 1777—just in time to raise a new corps of sharpshooters and to be sent off to join Horatio Gates in upper New York. At the Battle of Saratoga we see Morgan in his element, maneuvering his thin skirmish line of riflemen through the deep woods to fall on the unsuspecting British, calling them hither and yon with an eerie turkey gobble, orchestrating their movements like a conductor while they picked off enemy officers one by one from concealed positions in the dense forest.

Then, finally, came the battle that was all Morgan's—the classic demonstration of the resourceful frontiersman at his best, inventive, supremely practical, utilizing his

CONTINUED ON PAGE 97

Harper's Weekly, DECEMBER 12, 1874

AMERICAN HERITAGE BOOK SELECTION

PRELUDE TO WAR:
The Slaughter of the Buffalo

By JAMES L. HALEY

Although curiously neglected by historians, the Buffalo War of 1874–75 was, according to General Philip Sheridan, who engineered it, "the most successful of any Indian campaign in the country since its settlement by whites." By the end of it three of America's most powerful Indian tribes—the Cheyennes, the Kiowas, and the Comanches—had been subjugated, the bison had been exterminated from the South Plains, and white settlers could move freely into former Indian lands that stretched from central Kansas to central Texas.

By the terms of the Medicine Lodge Treaty, solemnly signed by the South Plains Indians in 1867, the United States government had pledged itself to protect the Indians from exactly such "successes" in return for the tribes' promises to move onto designated reservations. It was not the Indians who first broke the promises.

In a forthcoming book, The Buffalo War, *James L. Haley examines the intolerable pressures that forced the Indians back on the warpath at the tiny Texas town of Adobe Walls and along the Red River just seven years later. This thoughtful, disturbing book, from which the following article is adapted, will be published by Doubleday & Company next month.*

The train of events leading up to the Red River uprising begins three years after the treaty council at Medicine Lodge, in the fall of 1870, when a young New Englander named Josiah Wright Mooar came west and founded the

This 1874 Harper's Weekly *cover, "Slaughtered for the Hide," illustrated an angry story about the wanton killing of the buffalo.*

business of hunting buffalo for hides. Barely nineteen years old, blond, blue-eyed, just under six feet tall, he arrived in Fort Hays, Kansas, filled with visions of "the grandeur and dangers of the Wild West." The realities of the world caught up with him there, however, and he was obliged to support himself by the disappointingly unromantic job of supplying the local army post with wood, for which he was paid two dollars per cord. At Fort Hays he made friends with one James White, whose not too dissimilar task was to keep the post commissary stocked with meat. White was a buffalo hunter, and like all the others he took only the choice cuts, leaving the rest of the carcass, including the hide, lying on the prairie. White and the many other buffalo hunters on the Great Plains had made some noticeable inroads in the tremendous herds of buffalo, but still the animals numbered so many millions that they blanketed vast stretches of country.

Mooar and White often talked of the waste of skins, wondering if perhaps they would not be profitable as leather. A market had been growing back east for furry buffalo robes to use as sleigh blankets, for instance, and Indians had certainly tanned buffalo leather for centuries; but Mooar and White's idea remained merely speculation until an English firm made a contract with a Leavenworth, Kansas, robe and meat trader for five hundred hides. This company was interested in experimenting on the skins for tanning, and a subcontract fell to a hunter named Charlie Rath, who in turn contacted his friends, among them Wright Mooar. The youngster from Vermont fulfilled his part of the quota and found himself with a surplus of fifty-

COPYRIGHT © 1976 BY JAMES L. HALEY

The characters in this sad story are, from left to right: the hard-working Quaker agent at the Kiowa-Comanche reservation, James M. Haworth; the brothers who started the hide trade, John Wesley and Josiah Wright Mooar; Isa-tai, the Quahadi Comanche medicine man who instigated the uprising; Kiowa Chiefs Big Bow and Lone Wolf; Enoch Hoag, superintendent of the Indian Territory agencies; and John D. Miles, agent of the Cheyenne-Arapaho reservation.

seven hides; he sent the skins to his elder brother, John Wesley Mooar, in New York, to try to sell locally.

The hides were something of a novelty in New York, and they were to be put on display until they were purchased. Two tanners from Pennsylvania saw them being hauled down Broadway in an open wagon and later in the day called on the elder Mooar. They offered him $3.50 apiece for the hides, which Mooar accepted readily, and a few weeks later they contacted him again. They said they had experimented on the skins and were satisfied that they were useful, and inquired whether the Mooars would be interested in a contract for two thousand skins at $3.50 apiece, a total of seven thousand dollars. John Wesley instantly left New York for the Great Plains, and the Mooar brothers began hunting buffalo on a larger scale than anyone ever had before.

Though the Mooars started a couple of jumps ahead of the pack, the promise of easy, fast money to be had by preying upon the huge herds of buffalo attracted opportunists as surely as the rotting buffalo carcasses attracted flies; the business fairly exploded. Dodge City, Kansas, became the center of the trade, and perhaps the best records of the carnage were preserved by the commander of the local military post, Major Richard Irving Dodge: in 1873 alone the three rail lines serving Dodge City carried away over three quarters of a million hides, "exclusive of robes"; the figure for the three years 1872–74 totals an incredible 4,373,730 buffalo killed. That figure, said Dodge, was for the rail exports alone; other uses added at least a million more to the total.

Though the Indians to the south abhorred the wanton slaughter, they made no concerted move to stop it, as the depredations were confined to lands north of the Arkansas River. Land to the south of the Arkansas was considered Indian hunting ground, a limitation the hide hunters respected, at least in the early years of the Medicine Lodge Treaty. Their restraint was due principally to two factors: the abundance of buffalo still left in the north of Kansas and the ferocity of the Indians south of the Arkansas and in the Indian Territory.

William Blackmore, writing in 1877, recalled that

> in the autumn of 1868 [one year after the signing of the Medicine Lodge Treaty], whilst crossing the plains on the Kansas Pacific Railroad—for a distance of upwards of 120 miles, between Ellsworth and Sheridan [far to the north of the Arkansas River] we passed through an almost unbroken herd of buffalo. The plains were blackened with them, and more than once the train had to stop to allow unusually large herds to pass. A few years afterwards, when travelling over the same line of railroad, it was a rare sight to see a few herds of from ten to twenty buffalo.

In 1873 a plague of grasshoppers destroyed the settlers' crops in the Republican River Valley, again far to the north of the Arkansas. Although Mooar and the others had been in business only three years, when the Army sent several companies of troops to provide buffalo meat to keep the farmers from starving, they found to their great consternation that there were virtually no buffalo left. The Mooars and the swarms of buffalo hunters who followed them were doing their business with unbelievable efficiency. As far as the Arkansas River hunting boundary was concerned, William Blackmore went with an army scouting party on a trip along the Arkansas east of Fort Dodge in 1872. They

CREDITS, LEFT TO RIGHT: HAVERFORD COLLEGE LIBRARY, QUAKER COLLECTION, HAVERFORD, PA.; SCURRY COUNTY HISTORICAL MUSEUM, PICTURE DONATED BY DOT MOOAR, SNYDER, TEXAS; SCURRY COUNTY HISTORICAL MUSEUM, SNYDER, TEXAS; THE PANHANDLE-PLAINS HISTORICAL MUSEUM, CANYON, TEXAS; SMITHSONIAN INSTITUTION; THE PANHANDLE-PLAINS HISTORICAL MUSEUM, CANYON, TEXAS; THE OKLAHOMA HISTORICAL SOCIETY, OKLAHOMA CITY, OKLA.; THE OKLAHOMA HISTORICAL SOCIETY, OKLAHOMA CITY, OKLA.

found, he wrote later, "... a continuous line of putrescent carcasses, so that the air was rendered pestilential and offensive to the last degree. The hunters had formed a line of camps along the banks of the river, and had shot down the buffalo, night and morning, as they came to drink."

But none of the hunters dared cross the river, and the "dead line" (as it was called) held. For the first five years of the treaty (to 1872), to cross the Arkansas with buffalo guns and a wagon was to risk a horrible death at the hands of the Indians. A few desperate or greedy men did chance it, but then only in winter, when the Indians seldom left their camps, and with light, strong wagons and fast horses. And even then a number of them were picked off and scalped; it was obvious that the tribes of the South Plains had been driven back as far as they intended to go.

Only after the northern Kansas buffalo herds were gone did the hunters venture in force into the Indian hunting ground south of the Arkansas; they went down as far as, but rarely crossed, the boundary between the state of Kansas and the Indian Territory. In one season they mowed down the south Kansas buffalo like a scythe. On a scout from Dodge City to the Indian Territory, Blackmore recorded that "in 1872 ... we were never out of sight of buffalo. In the following autumn, while travelling over the same district, whilst the whole country was whitened with bleached and bleaching bones, we did not meet with buffalo until we were well into Indian country, and then only in scattered bands."

The suddenness of it all was appalling. Much as it strains today's imagination, the white men obliterated in one season's kill the south Kansas herds on which the Cheyennes and Arapahos had, in large measure, subsisted. The In-

Virtually this whole territory was denuded of its vast herds of buffalo by the hidemen within the three-year span 1872–1874.

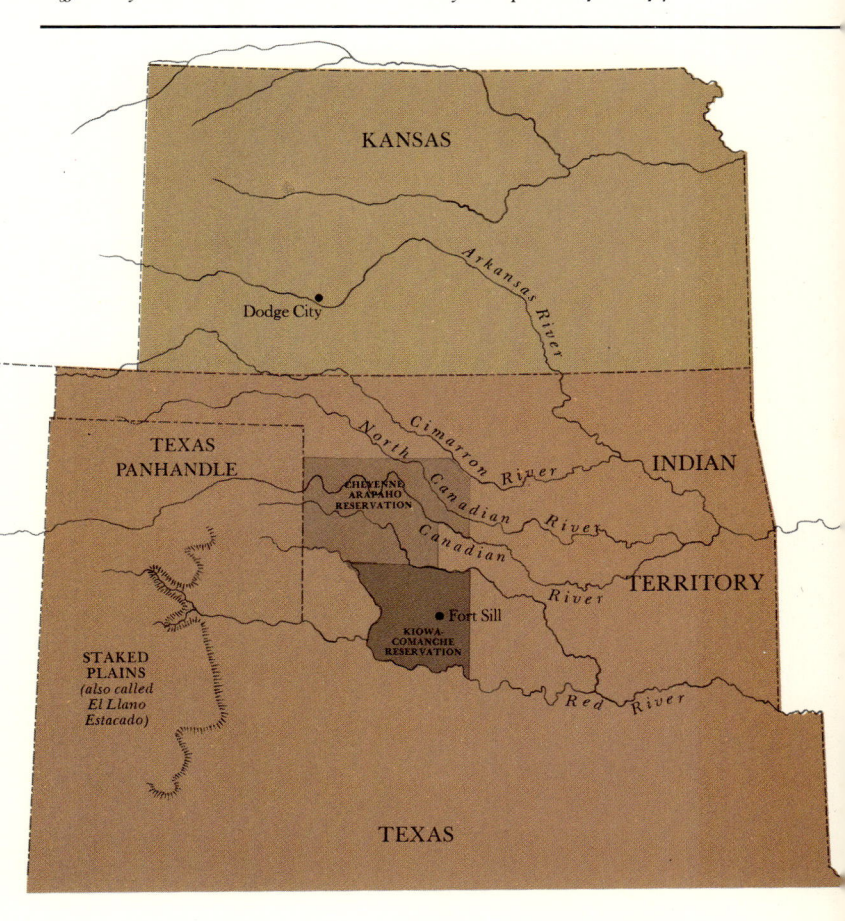

CAL SACKS

Like waves the great buffalo herds poured over the western plains, as in this painting, **Buffalo Herd on the Move** *by William J. Hayes.*

dians were powerless before the onslaught of an entire army of buffalo runners, as the hidemen called themselves, and had retreated to the sanctity of their reserve, where, the government promised them, white men would not—could not—follow. But follow they did, and with more alacrity than when they crossed the Arkansas. During the year the south Kansas buffalo were exterminated, Cheyenne and Arapaho war parties still managed to drive off those of the whites' hunting outfits that crossed the border into the "exclusive" domain of the Indians, but by the next year, 1873, raids on the Indians' stocks became more and more frequent, and the Indians, fighting now within their own territory, became less and less capable of fending off the tide of poachers.

Under the terms of the Medicine Lodge Treaty the United States Army was supposed to be patrolling the Kansas-Indian Territory boundary to see that nobody crossed. The troops were indeed watching over the border, but from an early date they had worked out a happy arrangement with the hunters to look the other way whenever the latter made a foray into the forbidden country. The prevalent view of the army men was best summed up by General Philip Sheridan when in 1875 he urged a session of the Texas legislature to defeat a conservation bill that would have preserved the buffalo from extinction. The hidemen "have done more in the last two years," he said,

> to settle the vexed Indian question than the entire regular army has done in the past thirty years. They are destroying the Indians' commissary . . . for the sake of lasting peace, let them kill, skin, and sell until the buffaloes are exterminated. Then your prairies can be covered with speckled cattle and the festive cowboy, who follows the hunter as a second forerunner of an advanced civilization.

As Phil Sheridan was the commander of the military division in which the slaughter was taking place, it seemed unlikely that the buffalo runners would meet any opposition from the Army; indeed, the soldiers enjoyed a buffalo hunt as much as anybody, and they did not even take the hides; they were just after the sport. As early as the campaigns of the 1860's the men under Colonel George A. Custer, operating as part of Sheridan's famous "winter campaign," divided into small squads to see which could kill the most buffalo in one day. Tallies were kept by cutting out the animals' tongues (later fed to camp dogs), and the rule was that the losers had to fix dinner for the others.

With the Army standing idly by, the "dead line," once accepted as the Arkansas River and then moved south to the border of the Indian Territory, was moved south yet again in 1873, on a de facto basis, all the way to the next large river south of the Arkansas, the Cimarron. That meant that the Indians had lost all control over what had been the reservation given them at Medicine Lodge, of which the Cimarron was the *southern* boundary. They were left to look for game in lands to the south and west.

For the voracious buffalo runners the 1873 killing season on the Cimarron was so successful that the Great Southern herd was depleted to the point where it would never again migrate north of the Canadian River, which at the Texas panhandle meridian is some one hundred miles *south* of the Cimarron. To gain any sense of the proportion of the slaughter one need only trace the carnage on a map: from the Arkansas to the border of the Indian Territory to the Cimarron to the Canadian, the prairies denuded of their thundering black herds and left silent and white, with millions of skeletons bleaching in the sun—all in the space of the three years 1872–74. The Indian tribes reeled before the juggernaut.

Totally heedless of what this would mean to the Indians, the hunters began to lay plans for the 1874 hunt on the Canadian. That, however, meant a hundred miles deeper penetration into the Indian Territory, a forbidding foray to even the bravest of them. Since none of them wished to isolate themselves in the middle of hostile Indian country, two of the plainsmen, Wright Mooar and John Webb, rode south of the territory into the panhandle of Texas, where very little hunting had ever been done except by the Comanche and Kiowa Indians, to investigate rumors that the prairies there were still grazed by huge and untouched herds of buffalo. Mooar and Webb did indeed find the herds and on their return reported that they had ridden through "an almost solid mass" of buffalo.

At this time, in the fall of 1873, the Kansas hunters began to worry that the Army might for once try to hinder their crossing Indian land, and sent emissaries in the persons of Wright Mooar and another hunter, Steele Frazier, to Major Dodge, the commander of Fort Dodge, whose job it was to patrol the border. Anxious to make a good impression on the major, Mooar and Frazier bathed (reputedly an extreme measure for a buffalo hunter) and wore brand-new

CONTINUED ON PAGE 82

And then the hidemen went to work. A mountainous pile of hides is stacked in the Rath Hide Yard in Dodge City, circa 1874.
KANSAS STATE HISTORICAL SOCIETY, TOPEKA

TRUE LOVE WILL OUT

The early-vintage cartoon strip above, dating back to about 1875, could well have used a few "balloons" of explanatory dialogue. As one follows it across the two pages a puzzling tale unfolds. A gentleman who treasures his peace and quiet is driven to distraction by an aspiring pianist. He plays a cruel prank with a hurdy-gurdy. Despairing of her talent, she abandons her art and her quarters; victorious, he leaps with joy. But wait! Life suddenly becomes leaden to him, and somehow he contrives to meet her again. Much is left unsaid, but the message is warm: love has again triumphed.

COLLECTION OF NORTON ASNER

44

MALLET, CHISEL, and CURLS

Vinnie Ream sculptured Lincoln while she was still a teen-ager

By STEPHEN W. STATHIS
and LEE RODERICK

President Lincoln had been dead more than three years in May of 1868, and the model of his statue still rested unfinished in young Vinnie Ream's Capitol studio. Now its very completion was threatened by a band of bitter congressmen who had failed to eject Mr. Lincoln's successor from the White House and, in their frustration, would try to turn Vinnie's ambition to ashes as well.

Vinnie Ream had come to Washington at the age of fourteen when her father, in 1861, found a job with the War Department's cartography section. It was an exciting place for a young girl, with soldiers constantly marching through the streets and ambulance vans from the nearby fighting front moving to army hospitals in the city. In the midst of the turmoil one recurring scene made an indelible impression on Vinnie. It was when the carriage bearing the tall, gaunt Mr. Lincoln would pass by, surrounded by a score of cavalrymen in colorful uniforms. Her fascination turned to a resolve to do a bust of the President. Soon the resolve became an obsession.

This portrait of Vinnie Ream was painted in her studio by George Caleb Bingham about 1876. By then she was already famous as the girl who had sculptured Lincoln.
STATE HISTORICAL SOCIETY OF MISSOURI, COLUMBIA

Between the pretty wisp of a girl—she weighed less than ninety pounds and was only about five feet tall—and her ambition there was a formidable array of obstacles. She was a mere youngster, reared in the prairie wilderness of Wisconsin, Kansas, and Missouri and unacquainted with the peculiar formal ways of official Washington. Although she had shown promise as an artist during a year's study at Christian College in Columbia, Missouri, she was still a beginner. And, in any event, Vinnie Ream was rather naive to believe that a wartime President had the time and patience for such a project.

These negative contemplations, however, were foreign to the nature of the spirited Miss Ream, who was not altogether unequipped for the challenge ahead. She had been endowed with a profusion of long, dark curls and bright, intelligent brown eyes. She also was gifted with a vivacious personality, which, combined with a certain amount of guile, sometimes opened doors in Washington that were closed to others.

The early months in the capital city were difficult ones financially for Robert Ream, and family members pitched in to help make ends meet. Vinnie's sister got a job in the land office; the family took in a former neighbor who was now a United States senator from Kansas, Edmund G. Ross, as a boarder; and Vinnie became a clerk at the post office.

It was while thus employed that Vinnie one day visited the studio of a noted American sculptor, Clark Mills. After watching Mills fashion a model, Vinnie, who had never tried sculpturing but was not one to underestimate her own ability, remarked to an escort: "I can do that myself." Overhearing the remark, Mills good-naturedly handed the girl a bucket of clay and challenged her to make good on her boast. Several weeks later the clay was returned to the studio, shaped convincingly into the head of an Indian. The result delighted Mills, who invited Vinnie to become his pupil-helper.

Under Mills's tutelage Vinnie's natural talent as a sculptor flowered swiftly into accomplishment, and she was soon able to leave the post office and devote her full energies to her art. Among the first famous Washingtonians who sat for a portrait bust by Vinnie was grim-faced Thaddeus Stevens of Pennsylvania. Stevens, the most powerful man in the House of Representatives, would later be chief architect of the scheme to impeach and destroy Andrew Johnson and—it would be charged—to destroy the constitutional role of the Executive as a coequal branch of

45

In the 1870's Vinnie Ream modelled a larger-than-life statue of Admiral David Glasgow Farragut, naval hero of the Civil War. It stands in Farragut Square, Washington, D.C.

the federal government.

True to Mills's influence, Vinnie's finished bust of Stevens was realistically accurate and did not soften the feared congressman's countenance. But Stevens expressed satisfaction with the result and remained from then on a steadfast friend to the young sculptor.

After Vinnie had worked with Mills for about a year, a sympathetic congressman approached President Lincoln to request permission for her to go to the White House for sittings while the great man worked at his desk. "Lincoln had been painted and modeled before," she would relate later, "and when friends of mine first asked him to sit for me he dismissed them wearily until he was told that I was but an ambitious girl, poor and obscure.... Had I been the greatest sculptor in the world I am sure that I would have been refused."

During the next five months, while war raged in the country, the little sculptor worked hard over her clay model of the President for a half hour each day. "I was the merest slip of a child... and the contrast between the rawboned man and me was indeed great," she remembered. "I sat demurely in my corner and begged Mr. Lincoln not to allow me to disturb him.... He seemed to find a strange sort of companionship in being with me, although we talked but little. His favorite son, Willie, had but just died, and this had been the greatest personal sorrow in a life that was mostly sorrowful. I made him think of Willie. He often said so and as often wept." Vinnie said she tried to capture in her model her strongest impression of Lincoln as a man "of unfathomable sorrow."

On April 14, 1865, Vinnie spent her usual half hour with Mr. Lincoln, working on the nearly complete model. The Union cause finally had gone well, and just five days earlier, after four bloody years of war, Lee had surrendered to Grant at Appomattox Courthouse to end the hostilities. No one could deny that the President needed diversion, and so it was on this evening that he had gone to Ford's Theatre to see *Our American Cousin.*

BOTH: LIBRARY OF CONGRESS

Vinnie was at the family home near Capitol Hill when the news came that shook the nation. Overwhelmed with sorrow at the assassination of her friend and hero, she was prostrated for days.

The shock to the stunned and still divided nation, which only with time would grasp fully the enormity of its loss, gradually gave way to a desire to memorialize properly America's martyred leader. One way, Congress decided, would be to commission a full-size statue of Mr. Lincoln to be placed in the Rotunda of the Capitol.

Although a competition was held for the coveted award, Vinnie had the inside track. During five years of Washington life she had learned her political lessons well, and four months before the commission was granted in August of 1866, a petition cogently attesting her competence was urged on prominent men in government.

In part, the "To Whom It May Concern" document read that the undersigned,

being personally acquainted with Miss Vinnie Ream, take great pleasure in endorsing her claims upon public patronage, no less as a most worthy and accomplished young lady, than as possessing rare genius in the beautiful art of sculpture. ... We feel every confidence that she will excel in her profession, and, with age and experience, rank her name with those who have already won high places in America's temple of art.

The first two signatures on the petition were those of President Andrew Johnson and General Ulysses S. Grant. The name of Edmund Ross headed a list of thirty-one senators, and that of Thaddeus Stevens a hundred and ten members of the House.

The contract called for five thousand dollars to be paid Vinnie upon completion of the plaster model and five thousand dollars upon completion and acceptance of the finished marble statue. It was the first time that Congress had commissioned a woman to execute sculpture for the government. For good measure, the somewhat infatuated Congress threw in a studio in the Capitol, rent-free, which soon became a favorite Capitol Hill attraction for the curious who had heard romantic tales of the wonder girl from the West, still not twenty years old.

Vinnie understandably drew more than her share of jealous detractors, who were not to be silenced by her *fait accompli*. For example, a newspaper columnist, Mrs. Jane Grey Swisshelm, vented her irritation in an article describing how Vinnie "carries the day" with members of Congress:

Miss .... Ream ... is a young girl of about twenty who has been studying her art for a few months, never made a statue, has some plaster busts on exhibition, including her own, minus clothing to the waist, has a pretty face, long dark curls and plenty of them. ... [She] sees members at their lodgings or in the reception room at the Capitol, urges her claims fluently and confidently, sits in the galleries in a conspicuous position and in her most bewitching dress, while those claims are being discussed on the floor, and nods and smiles as a member rises. ...

An editor had the last word, however, when he printed her column under the headline "A Homely Woman's Opinion of a Pretty One."

Later less biassed critics, while acknowledging Vinnie's native talent, would fault Congress for awarding the important commission to one so unschooled. And the more thoughtful among Vinnie's contemporary admirers worried over the dangers of the flattery that was being heaped upon her. "While it might, in some degree, cheer and encourage," wrote a correspondent in the *Overland Monthly* of August, 1871, "it was calculated to stifle study and effort, under the impression that there was little more to learn, and to leave the girl to be satisfied with half-way excellence." Vinnie brushed off this concern with an answer that belied her age: "These people know nothing whatever of art. I had rather have the opinions of one even merciless judge than the unmeaning, but well-meant, praise of all of them."

Vinnie set to work on the clay model, her goal now in sight. The sculptor's pleasant studio, located adjacent to the crypt of the Capitol, directly below the Rotunda, was convenient to the family home, and her life was both uncomplicated and fulfilling.

While Vinnie was absorbed in the important task at hand over the next two years, the country outside her studio, and the Senate and House above it, debated momentous issues that the nation vainly hoped had been resolved at Appomattox. Abraham Lincoln's untimely death had removed from the scene the one man who might have commanded enough respect to heal the wounds still festering between North and South and to somehow appease Northerners thirsting to further

CONTINUED ON PAGE 94

Vinnie's principal claim to fame: her marble statue of Lincoln, unveiled in 1871

47

THE DON QUIXOTE OF OPERA

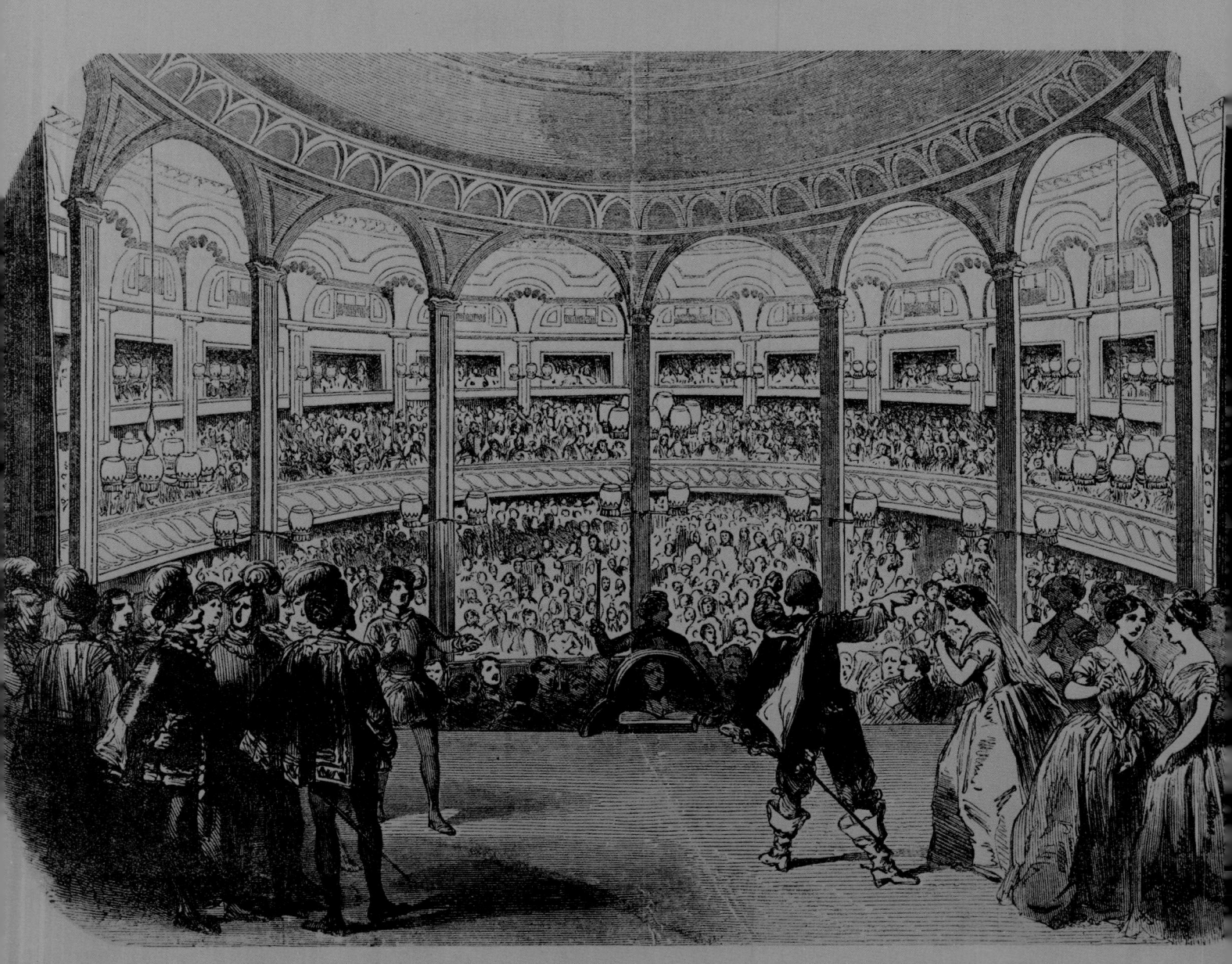

It was Maretzek's dream to bring opera to the common man by hiring the huge Castle Garden Theatre in New York's Battery Park and filling the five thousand seats at fifty cents each. The project was launched for the 1854 season, but did not work out altogether as planned. Above is an artist's conception of how Castle Garden looked from stage rear in the middle of a Maretzek-produced operatic performance.

HARVARD THEATRE COLLECTION

*No other impresario ever matched the record
of the indomitable Max Maretzek in bringing
new works and new stars to America*

He was called "the indomitable Max," "the indefatigable Max," "the hardy pioneer," "the Napoleon of Opera." About that Napoleonic designation Max Maretzek himself disagreed. It would be more accurate, he ruefully said, if he were described as the Don Quixote of Opera. And in a way he was right. For some forty years the indomitable, indefatigable Max tilted at the American public and at assorted singers, mostly Italian, making and losing fortunes in the process. A stout, ebullient, eternally optimistic man, a good musician, a canny infighter when he had to be, a gambler, he was in many respects the Sol Hurok of his day, and he did more to establish opera in general and Italian opera in particular in the United States during the period before and after the Civil War than any other man.

This was recognized by all, and even his enemies paid tribute to his work. Maretzek had his share of enemies in the press and in the business, but he was always good copy, never reticent in talking about himself, and he had almost a Hurok-like ability to identify himself with his product. The American public followed his ups and downs with fascination. The press gave credit where credit was due. As early as 1855 the *New York Times* was referring to Max as "the hero of nineteen opera campaigns." "Seven years ago," said the *Times*, "he landed in America with nothing but talent and a wooden baton.

Today he has nothing but talent and a wooden baton." Max had just lost a fortune on a low-priced opera project. In Boston, *Dwight's Journal of Music* referred to him as "the hardworking protagonist of the Italian opera.... To Mr. Maretzek, New York is indebted for much of its best musical education." The same kind of comment was echoed by the New York *World* in 1858: "No man has done so much for operatic music."

There was not much opera in New York when Max Maretzek arrived in 1848. Indeed, New York had never even been exposed to the art until 1825, when a company headed by Manuel García came from London to give a season at the Park Theatre. In the 1830's there was an attempt to establish opera in the city, but so much money was lost that very few attempts were made in the next decade. In 1847, however, the Astor Place Opera House was built, and that is where Maretzek came in.

Maretzek, born in Moravia (now Czechoslovakia) on June 28, 1821, had studied music in Vienna. He developed into a composer and conductor. Indeed, at the age of nineteen he composed an opera, *Hamlet*, which had a bit of a run. He settled in Paris as a conductor, became friendly with Berlioz, Meyerbeer, Liszt, and other heroes of the romantic movement, and then moved to Her Majesty's Theatre in Covent Garden. There he was choral director and assistant conductor. It was in 1848 that he came to the attention of Edward P. Fry, an American impresario who was looking for talent for the new Astor Place Opera House. Fry asked Maretzek to come over as chief conductor, and the adventuresome Max jumped at the chance. Every European knew that the streets of New York were paved with gold. Max arrived at his El Dorado in September, 1848, and almost immediately started putting his mark on the musical life of the country.

The most complete account of his adventures reposes in his two autobiographical volumes—*Crochets and Quavers* (1855) and *Sharps and Flats* (1890). Considering his importance and popularity it is surprising that there has been no biography or other full-fledged study. There is not even a scholarly study of any kind, and anybody interested in his doings has to leaf through newspapers and magazines of his day. There plenty can be encountered to supplement—and correct—the often imaginative exploits recounted in his own books. There is, incidentally, something of a mystery about those two volumes. Max soon became fluent enough in English, but not so fluent that in 1855 he could turn out the amusing, highly idiomatic, combative prose that makes *Crochets and Quavers* such a delight. Max admits as much. He says that while working on the book he "rushed from the world," secluded himself in his Staten Island home "with an English Grammar, an Eng-

By HAROLD C. SCHONBERG

lish Dictionary, and an English friend," and made up his mind "with the assistance of these three indispensable necessaries to my task, to attempt its completion." Nobody knows who the English friend was. Whoever he may have been, he was a first-class ghostwriter. Yet a spirit that can have come from nowhere but the mind of Max animates the book.

It has to be taken with a grain of salt, of course. Max was naturally interested in presenting his side of any particular case, and he wrenches a few facts here and there while doing so. With his natural ebullience and feeling for the ridiculous, too, he often veers into sheer burlesque, especially when gleefully describing the personal and musical shortcomings of his singers. Could *anything* be as inept as some of the performances he describes? But History whispers "Yes." The mid-nineteenth-century operatic scene in New York, with its hastily assembled casts, its pampered leading singers, its skimpy rehearsals, and its poorly trained orchestras was an example of the lyric stage in extremis. Certainly the spectacle upon which Maretzek gazed on his arrival—even discounting his tendency to exaggerate—was cosmic humor of a sort that has passed from the earth.

The twenty-seven-year-old conductor arrived in September, 1848, and the first impression he received was one that will wrench a sigh from New Yorkers of the 1970's: "I was immediately struck with the beauty of the Bay and its environs. That which principally delighted me was, however, its bright, clear and blue sky. Such a sky I had not seen since I last left Naples." He looked around, settled in, and went to the Astor Place Opera House to observe a performance of *Il Barbiere di Siviglia*. He was, to say the least, not very impressed. The orchestra did not even have a conductor. As in the old days, the conducting, such as it was, devolved upon the concertmaster. This concertmaster, while playing, "trampled on the floor as though he had been determined to work a path through the deal planking, and made a series of . . . grotesque faces." The trampling was to give the rhythm to the players, but nobody was looking at the concertmaster, and his tramplings were ignored. The other string players scraped away, producing sounds resembling those of a sawmill in full operation. Every musician in the orchestra "went his own way, and made his own speed." It was chaos. As for the singers, "it became unmistakably evident to me that none of them would ever produce a revolution in the musical world."

Max later goes into a description of his singers in some detail, concentrating on the tenors. Many years

Max Maretzek as he looked in 1849

later Frances Alda was to write a book named *Men, Women and Tenors*; and Giulio Gatti-Casazza, manager of the Metropolitan Opera, would tap his noble brow when anything went wrong and say, with infinite significance, "The head of a tenor." Everybody in the business knows that tenors are a breed apart, followed closely by the prima donnas and then by all other musicians. Max spent many years wondering about and marvelling at the antics of musicians. He professed to be puzzled by the fact that musicians are the most quarrelsome of all beings upon the face of God's round earth—that members of the most harmonious of all professions should be its most inharmonious set of denizens.

The leading singers for Maretzek's 1848–49 season were a Signora Truffi, the tenor Sesto Benedetti, and the bass Settimo Rosi. Truffi, said Max, was a competent but not very exciting soprano. Benedetti was "as cunning as either a monk or a weasel." He had a strong voice and a total lack of musical culture. "Did he chance to sing a false note, or commit an error in intonation, he would look daggers at some unoffending member of the orchestra." That type is around to this day. Benedetti also had other jokers in his deck. "Whenever he could not keep time, he had the trick of beginning to beat it himself, although he literally never knew the difference between a six-eight and a two-four movement. This was for the purpose of showing the audience that the fault, supposing they discerned it, lay with the conductor." As for Signor Rosi, his idea of acting was "to draw a long breath, put himself into a fighting attitude, and then rush to the footlights." We still have *those* today, too.

It was a season that proved the theatrical theorem that anything that could happen would happen. There was an *Ernani* in New York with a cast of new and untried singers gathered together by Fry. The bass was Salvatore Castrone. He made a grand entrance, tripped over his sword, and rolled into a group of terrified choristers. Then he got his spurs tangled in the prima donna's gown. After which, paralyzed with fright, he planted himself in front of the prompter's box and simply refused to move for the rest of the act. Later in the opera he had troubles of another sort. When he wanted to draw his sword, it stuck in the scabbard. When he did get it out, he never was able to sheathe it, desperately poking this way and that to find the aperture of the scabbard. If he was supposed to enter stage right, he entered stage left, surprising the whole company. When he knelt, he split his costume. Then . . . then . . .

But let Max tell the story. In the last act the wretched Castrone rushed on stage:

He . . . had forgotten what the Erse or

Northern Scotch, though which it is I have suffered myself to forget, call their "gallygaskins." In our own more fastidiously refined language, upon this continent, they are most generally and generically classified as the "unmentionables." There he stood, representing the Spanish idea of an Inexorable Fate, clad in a black velvet doublet, but with a pair of flesh-colored and closely-woven silk inexpressibles upon his nether man. The horn, that fatal horn, hung from his neck in a position which it would be absolutely impossible for me consistently with propriety to indicate upon paper. Certainly, it was in anything but its right place. Some of the ladies who were present rose and quitted the theater. Others shrank back in their seats and veiled their eyes. . . .

At the end of the season Maretzek was offered the company. He took it over, leased the Astor Place Opera House for twelve thousand dollars annually, got together a troupe, and was in business for himself—as he was to be for the next thirty and more years. In the troupe was a soprano named Bertucca. Maretzek shortly afterward married her. After her voice went, she played the harp in the orchestra and also did solo work on that instrument.

The doughty Max spread himself wide, meeting crisis after crisis with aplomb, taking on the competition as it appeared, jousting with the press. The *New York Times* on the whole supported his work, but the *Tribune* took out after him. Max was convinced that the *Tribune* critic, William Henry Fry, was hostile because he, Max, did not stage his opera. William Henry Fry, the brother of the Edward Fry who had brought Maretzek to the United States, did write the first opera ever composed by an American—*Leonora*, staged in Philadelphia in 1845. But Maretzek had a low opinion of Fry as a critic. Fry, he said, "uses in every ten or a dozen words some four or five technical expressions. By this simple means, he has the satisfaction of rendering his writing unintelligible to the general reader, while it is of no service to the practical musician."

Max not only took on Fry, he also fought the *Tribune* editorial staff and the terrible-tempered publisher, James Gordon Bennett himself. When

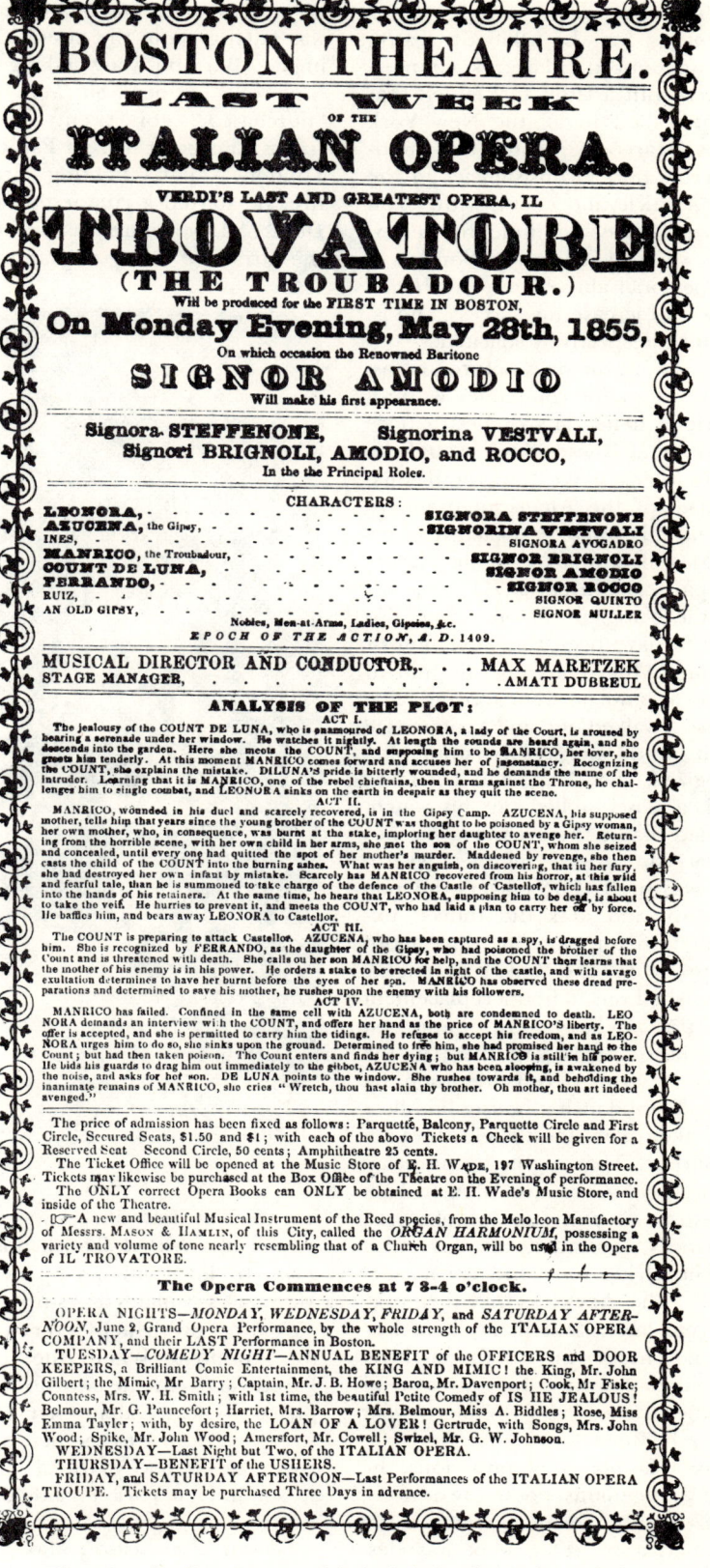

Though a leading Boston critic had furiously condemned Il Trovatore *in New York, Maretzek boldly took it to Boston.*
BOTH: HARVARD THEATRE COLLECTION

the *Tribune* attacked Maretzek after his singers for the 1866–67 season were announced, Maretzek counter-attacked with a letter to Bennett that was published in all the New York papers. Maretzek pointed out multiple errors and inconsistencies in the *Tribune* article and ended with: "You may, therefore, continue for a few more years your opposition.... A little personal abuse from the *Herald* may even increase my success, and is, therefore, respectfully solicited."

Those were the days before unions, and Max ran his companies with an imperious hand. His orchestra once pulled what these days would be called a wildcat strike. It was at the final rehearsal of the American première of Donizetti's *Maria di Rohan*. It seems that Max had rebuked some players with particular asperity. He was not only the Napoleon of opera; he also seems to have been the Toscanini of his time. This rehearsal saw him in fine form, and he went too far. The orchestra walked out, and a committee said it would not return until Max apologized. So Napoleon-Toscanini struck a pose, pulled out his watch, and said that if the orchestra was not in place in fifteen minutes, everybody was fired. The players did not show up, and Max did indeed immediately fire them. But what about the première the following night? Max rushed out to find a replacement orchestra. "They were impressed everywhere. We seized them in the streets. Descents were made upon the highly moral dancing-houses. Fiddlers were taken from the vessels of war in the harbor. That night, no musician was secure." At 5 A.M. Max had an orchestra. At 7 it was in rehearsal. Rehearsals continued all day, with Max supplying food and encouragement. "The key [to the theatre]," he wrote later, "was in my breeches' pocket. There was not the slightest possibility of escape for any one of them." At 8 P.M. the première went on as scheduled.

Max was not only imperious; he could be ingenious, not to say devious. When Barnum brought Jenny Lind to America in 1850, Max was desperate. He knew that he would have trouble attracting an audience to his opera presentations; everybody was talking about the Swedish Nightingale. Barnum was making a fortune out of her. So Max quickly "purchased," for twenty thousand francs, the great Teresa Parodi from London. Then, fighting fire with fire, he started a rumor that the old Duke of Devonshire was lusting after the attractive young soprano. America, then as now, always was titillated by the life-style of British nobility. A *duke*! In love with an opera singer! Maretzek's planted stories were picked up by virtually every paper in the country. When the innocent Parodi arrived, she was no little surprised to learn about her love life. Everybody came to see her, and Max rode the publicity for a profitable season in New York, Philadelphia, and Boston.

Season after season Max gathered unto himself a company and introduced America to the operas of Verdi, Donizetti, and many others. In the fall of 1850 he took command of a company that had come from Havana. This was an eye opener. Never before had he encountered a group of singers with equivalent jealousies, intrigues, and pettiness. Much of this, Max believed, could be traced to stage husbands. If there was one thing Max hated more than operatic tenors,

The opera house offered a lively scene at performance time. Both of these views show the Philadelphia Academy of Music, where Maretzek was in charge for several years.

it was the stage husband. One of his leading sopranos, Angelina Bosio, had a husband who rejoiced in the wonderful name of Signor Panayotis di Xindavelonis. Max watched him aghast. Xindavelonis' mission in life was to impress his wife with his usefulness and importance. He would see that her soup was hot and her champagne cold. He would dutifully carry her poodle under one arm and her music under the other. He would argue with conductors about the tempos in her arias, though he knew as much about tempos as did the poodle under his arm. He would pick fearsome arguments over trifles so that his wife would think he had saved her from artistic ruin.

In that company was a tenor named Lorenzo Salvi, with whom Max was to be associated for many years. Salvi, like so many tenors, was a little crazy. Max firmly believed that Salvi thought himself to be the Louis Quatorze of opera. "*L'opéra, c'est moi!*" One of Salvi's cuter tricks was to insist on a contract containing a provision to the effect that in case of illness there were to be fourteen days of grace. Sure enough, if Salvi did not feel like singing, his servant would come to Max with a medical certificate "certifying to an attack of bronchitis, yellow fever, or cholera morbus." Thus for thirteen days Salvi had a vacation with full pay. Then he would sing. On the following day he would have a relapse—unless the manager humbled himself and got down on his knees.

It is the job of an impresario to learn to handle this kind of nonsense. Salvi had a good voice, and popular tenors are always in a position to pamper their lusty egos. Max put up with Salvi and the others; he had to; there was no other option. But it was hard, hard. It was Salvi who in 1853 ruined Maretzek's benefit. In those days it was the custom for certain nights of the season to be given for the benefit of the manager, who would take all the proceeds, pay off the major outstanding debts, and perhaps pocket a few surplus dollars. The Maretzek benefit was scheduled for December 19, 1853. Salvi suddenly decided, the afternoon of the concert, that he wanted his fee in advance. Max, the last one to submit to blackmail, closed down Niblo's Garden instead. The *New York Times* did some digging and learned that Salvi was in debt and being dunned. Among the debts was $253.00 "to the druggist Dubuic for 80 gallons of cod liver oil." Tenors are eccentric folk, but it was the general feeling that 80 *gallons* of cod-liver oil was carrying things a bit far. What on earth did Salvi do? Bathe in it? (It later was found that he had purchased it for delivery to Italy.) The *Times* pointed out that in the previous twenty months Max had paid Salvi "upwards of thirty thousand dollars." Was Salvi worth it? The *Times* thought no. "Signor Salvi cannot be ranked with the first tenors of the present day, except by a traditional and extremely unsatisfactory fiction. He is *passé* and tolerated simply because he is one of the best we have among us."

Salvi was one member of a strong company with which Max all but ruined himself in 1854. He got the idea of giving a season of low-priced opera—fifty cents admission for all seats—at Castle Garden in Battery Park. Such prices, he thought, would popularize opera. And as Castle Garden had about five thousand seats, there even was the possibility of a hefty profit. (Five thousand seats in those days before electronic amplification! The singers were a leather-lunged breed.) "Dreaming a golden dream," Max wrote, "I fancied that with such a Company as this actually was, with prices no higher than the regular theatrical ones, and a large house, the taste for Italian Opera might be established, not amongst the 'Upper Ten,' but in the public heart of New York." Alas! The company found itself playing to audiences of a hundred or a hundred and fifty, scarcely enough to meet the printing bills. Max ended up with a $22,000 deficit.

Max bounced back. He always did. Wherever there was opera, there was Max. He took a troupe to Mexico and made money. He competed with new impresarios. One of those was an immigrant named Max Strakosch, and the "war of the Maxes" enlivened and amused New York for many years. Great singers started coming to the United States, sometimes with their own companies. In 1853 New York could enjoy a company headed by Henrietta Sontag and another headed by Marietta Alboni. Sontag was one of the all-time greats. She had been a favorite artist of Carl Maria von Weber (creating the title role in *Euryanthe*) and was admired by Beethoven (she was the soprano in the world premières of the Ninth Symphony and the *Missa Solemnis*). Max worked out a deal with Alboni for a short season at Niblo's Garden and then contracted with Sontag for a summer season at Castle Garden.

53

Thomas Nast's 1873 cartoon celebrated the battle between Maretzek and Max Strakosch to outstar each other that season in New York opera.

BOTH: HARVARD THEATRE COLLECTION

Max always had his eye to the main chance. Poor Sontag, incidentally, did not have much longer to live. She contracted cholera while on a tour of Mexico the following year.

In 1854 the Academy of Music on Fourteenth Street near Third Avenue was built, and Max took it over the following year. One of his achievements was the preparation of the American première of *Il Trovatore*. The public loved it, but not John Sullivan Dwight in Boston. Dwight came to New York for the première and also attended all performances when the company played Boston. His stern Unitarian heart almost stopped beating. What was opera coming to? Dwight took off on *Il Trovatore* in his *Journal of Music*. He could find nothing new in the work, nothing that showed any progress. The opera demonstrated "only a hardened habit in the old false way; —the way of substituting strong, glaring and intense *effects*, at whatsoever cost of theme and treatment for the real inspirations of sincere human life and feeling."

There was a trip to Havana. Maretzek decided that since Havana had been without opera from 1853 to 1856, "the señoritas began to grow tired of toreadors and were longing for sweet tenors, and the caballeros, satiated with the blood of bulls and horses, were clamoring for prima donnas and ballerinas." So Maretzek whipped together a company, chief among which was the baritone Signor Amodio.

Amodio had a fresh, appealing voice. He also weighed "about 300 pounds, with a body like a Heidelberg wine cask surmounted by the head of a young boy." As soon as the company disembarked, Amodio was the center of attraction, especially when he entered a carriage and went right through the floorboards. "The horse, frightened by the shock, started, and Amodio, with his head above and his feet below the *volante*, had to run under a scorching sun about six blocks in the Calle Obispo, among repeated cheers and screams of the following crowd, until at last rescued by the police.... From that day until the end of the season, whenever Amodio approached a stand of *volantes*, there was a general stampede among the black drivers, who stoutly refused to carry and to have their *volantes* broken by that monster."

Amodio was promptly nicknamed *el niño gordo*—the fat baby—and every performance in which he sang was sold out. All Havana wanted to see

In mid-career Maretzek was caricatured as hawking a rich assortment of prima donnas.

him. Maretzek even ordered him to dance a tarantella in "Masaniello," and Amodio, a good sport, did so, to universal applause.

One thing Maretzek liked about Havana: the authorities stood no nonsense from singers. That made Havana the promised land for an operatic manager. If a singer reported in sick, the police would send a physician. If the physician could find nothing wrong with the singer—no fever, no inflammation of the throat, no swelling of the vocal cords—and if the singer still refused to appear, a corporal and four soldiers were sent to escort him to the theatre "and there leave him the choice of advancing toward the stage before him, or retreating with four bayonets behind him."

A return trip to Mexico proved a financial disaster. The great Adelina Patti promised Maretzek that she would be part of the company in Mexico. Maretzek immediately promised the Mexican public they would have Patti. But the prima donna finally changed her mind, at which point the Mexican public changed its mind about Maretzek's company. The refunds were enough to make the goddess of music weep for very pity. Maretzek persevered, running into robbers, coming down with fever, borrowing money to pay his singers, and arriving home with exactly six dollars in his pocket. "After paying my hotel bill that night I reached my home on Staten Island absolutely penniless." Six months later he was in business again, running a New York season with the best company he had ever had.

Now and then Maretzek worked outside of New York. There was a three-year period when he was head of the new Academy of Music in Philadelphia while Maurice Strakosch (Max Strakosch's brother) and Bernard Ullmann ran the Academy of Music in New York. Back in New York in 1860, Maretzek took over the Winter Garden Theatre and then resumed direction of the Academy of Music. The building was destroyed by fire in 1866. Unbowed, Max promptly announced a season for 1867 and set to work raising money to rebuild the house. Said the *Times*, admiringly, when the new Academy of Music opened over the ashes of the old one: "A great loser by the fire and its unavoidable results, Maretzek held on to his company, engaged new artists, and before the smoke had ceased curling above the blackened walls of his ruined temple, reorganized his troupe and laid plans for the coming season." To celebrate the reopening there was a promenade concert—an opera ball, as Max called it. Three New York

55

orchestras were engaged for the Saturday afternoon event, and the program tells a good deal about the popular tastes of the day:

1. March from Meyerbeer's *Le Prophète*
2. Potpourri from Meyerbeer's *L'Africaine*
3. Wagner's *Rienzi* Overture
4. Valse, *Le Guard*
5. Selection, *Ione* [an opera by Enrico Petrella that Maretzek had introduced to America in 1863]
6. Trio, *Crespino e la Comare*
7. *Yacht Club Waltz* [composed for the occasion]
8. Selections from Donizetti's *Gemma di Vergy*
9. Suppé's *Poet and Peasant* Overture
10. Selection from Meyerbeer's *Robert le Diable*
11. *Jockey Club* Gallop [composed for the occasion]
12. Aria from Verdi's *Nabucco*
13. Potpourri from Gounod's *Faust*
14. *Marien* Gallop
15. *Six-in-Hand* Lancers
16. *Musical Telegraph*
17. Potpourri of Marches
18. Medley

Said the *New York Times* of this program: "The music could not be more choice."

There was great excitement in 1872 when Maretzek brought Pauline Lucca to his company. She was one of the important sopranos of Europe, and she lived up to her reputation. Maretzek alternated her with the famous American soprano Clara Louise Kellogg. Even more exciting was the 1873 season, when Maretzek had Enrico Tamberlik and Ilma di Murska in addition to Lucca and Kellogg. For this Max took over the Grand Opera House at 114 Broadway. Tamberlik may have seen his best days by then, but he was still an imposing stentorian tenor; and his high C and even C sharp rang out as brilliantly as ever. (It was not a high register to everybody's liking. Tamberlik once asked permission from Rossini to visit. Rossini, whose ideal of singing was flexible bel canto, who hated high notes and loud attacks, told Tamberlik that he would be happy to receive him, but would he kindly check his high C sharp with the concierge.)

Max did not have many years left as an impresario. He was growing a bit old, was losing his zest, and times were changing. Strakosch and the others—the most formidable new entrant was an energetic Englishman named James Mapleson—were providing too much competition, and Maretzek was regarded as old-fashioned. It was not that Maretzek and Strakosch could not get along. Maretzek may have attacked Strakosch professionally, and gave some sizzling interviews about him, but they were really comrades-in-arms and could work together. Strakosch sometimes engaged Maretzek as conductor for his own companies. New York observers were amused. A strange combination, wrote one critic, "one day engaged in pitched battle, the next day walking arm in arm along Fourteenth Street, discussing some prodigious scheme to bring them nearer to bankruptcy than they both already were." At one time Strakosch had a company with such international headliners as Alice Nilsson, Italo Campanini, Joseph Capoul, and Victor Maurel—the same season that Maretzek was offering Tamberlik and Lucca.

No wonder both went broke in this opera war. Maretzek believed that Strakosch was irresponsible. Strakosch was even more of a plunger than Maretzek was, and he just about put his rival out of business by paying his leading singers outlandish fees. Then when Maretzek's singers learned what Strakosch was paying, they would not return until those fees were matched. Strakosch was paying his leading sopranos four thousand dollars a week, his leading tenors two thousand, other singers four to six hundred dollars. The whole orchestra those days could be hired for fifteen hundred dollars weekly; a chorus, eleven hundred; and the house rental was three thousand dollars.

After a short season at the Academy of Music in 1875, Max Maretzek retired as an impresario. For a while he was missed; New York musical life was not the same with him gone. "Max Maretzek," announced the *Herald* in 1877, "to whom New York owes so much for good opera, is compelled to teach to eke out a livelihood, but he is looking younger and fresher than in his halcyon days." Perhaps Max stopped every now and then to think of his past accomplishments. What a record he had compiled! In his thirty-odd years as an opera impresario he had been responsible for a list of American premières that no other manager in the history of music in America has come near. Thanks to Maretzek the United States heard for the first time the following Donizetti operas: *Betly, Il Poliuto, Maria di Rohan,* and *Don Sebastiano.* Verdi operas introduced by Max were *La Traviata, Rigoletto, Il Trovatore, La Forza del Destino, Attila, Aroldo, Luisa Miller,* and *I Masadnieri.* Meyerbeer's *Le Prophète, L'Africaine,* and *Étoile du Nord* were presents from Max. So were *Mignon* by Ambroise Thomas, *Roméo et Juliette* by Gounod, *L'Ombra* by Flotow, *Saffo* and *Medea* by Pacini, and *Duchess of Amalfi* and *Ione* by Petrella. This is at best a partial list; the records are untabulated, and exhaustive research should turn up many more.

Besides setting himself up as a teacher and vocal coach, Maretzek also resumed composing. He finished an opera called *Sleepy Hollow,* which had its world première at the Academy of Music on September 25, 1879. The *Times* called it an opera of "decided merit . . . nothing sleepy or hollow about it." Maretzek took out advertisements after the first night: IMMEDIATE AND COLOSSAL SUCCESS! NEARLY EVERY NUMBER REDEMANDED! ALL THE SCENES ENCORED! UNANIMOUS FAVORABLE VERDICT OF THE PUBLIC! After which it is with a sense of anticlimax that one looks at the New York newspapers of October 5 and reads the following notice:

Notwithstanding the gratifying and nightly increasing artistic success of American opera, the financial result has been so far such as to confirm the unanimous opinion of the press and public that the Academy of Music is not the proper place to risk English or American opera. Under these circumstances, the management feels justified in discontinuing the performances for the present. Arrangements are pending for its revival elsewhere.—Max Maretzek.

But there was to be no revival,

CONTINUED ON PAGE 97

Artists of the Santa Fe

The Atchison, Topeka and Santa Fe Railway grew in a cloud of violence that quickly became legendary. Wherever the fledgling railroad went in the 1870's, it left a raw and brawling cow town in its wake. At the Colorado ranges gunplay broke out between the work crews of the Santa Fe and the rival Denver & Rio Grande. By the 1890's this inaugural roughhousing had subsided, leaving the Santa Fe with a right-of-way that passed through some of the most beautiful landscape in creation, and a nation full of potential customers who, having heard the stories, were afraid to go and see it. This was the problem confronting W. H. Simpson when he established the railroad's advertising department in 1896. His job was to alert people to the thundering scenery of the Santa Fe route, and it is not surprising that he lit on the idea of having artists paint it and then using their works in colorful promotion calendars and posters. What is surprising is the scope and success of the project. A few artists had already established themselves in New Mexico, drawn to the highly picturesque town of Taos at the base of a mountain that rose up five thousand feet through air clear as gin. The railroad approached them and soon began to supply transportation and lodgings for other painters who would journey to the Southwest. The Santa Fe printed its first advertising calendar in 1907 and thereafter was chief among the very few early patrons of western art. In time the collection grew to a total of 553 paintings. Of these, more than two hundred feature the Indians of the Southwest. The one above, by Lon Megargee, is entitled *Navajos Watching Santa Fe Train*. It and its fellows provide an impressive glimpse of ancient cultures that were disappearing even as the artists recorded them. We herewith present the first published portfolio of the Santa Fe Collection of Southwestern Art.

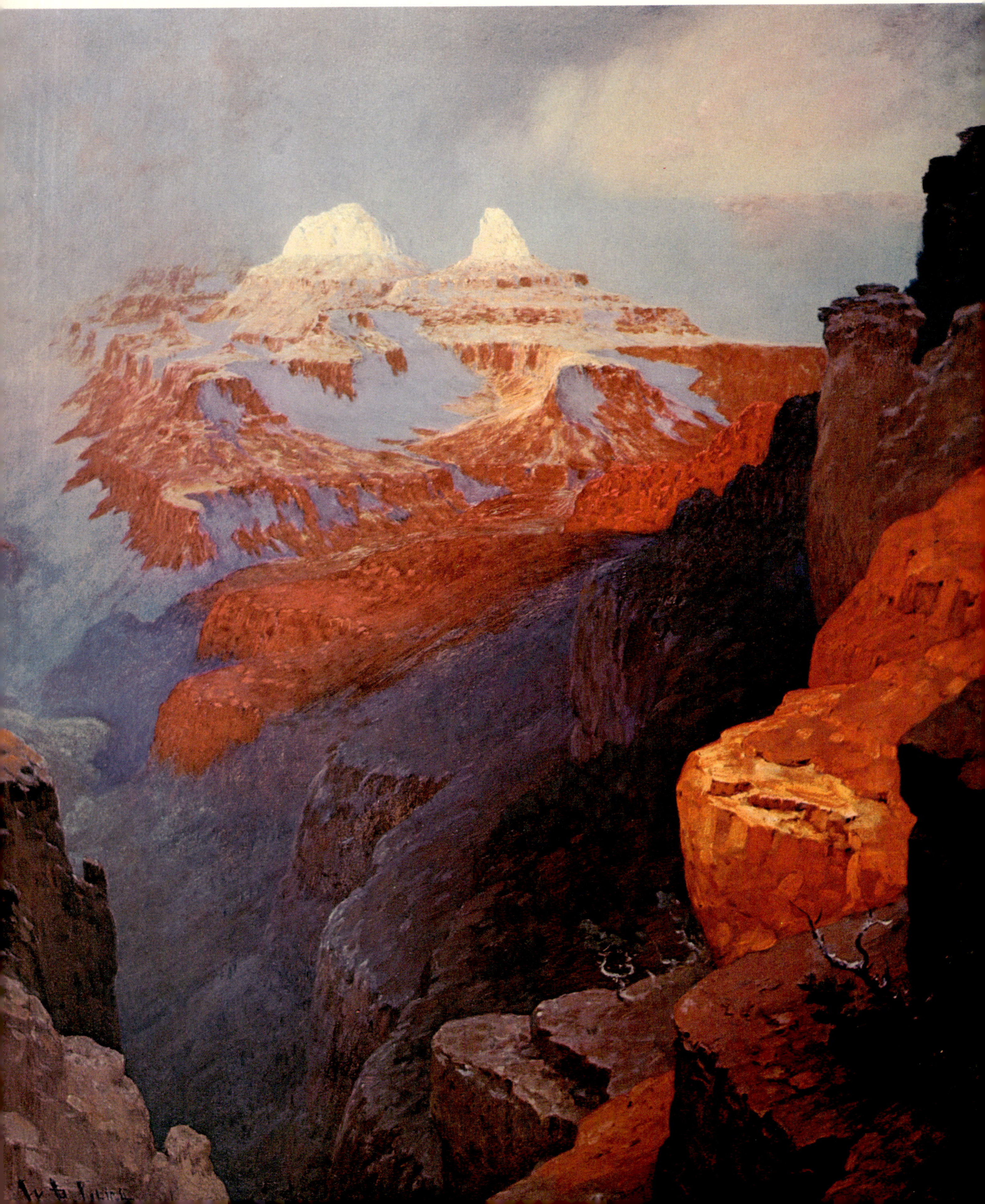

"Never in the whole of human history, at any time or anywhere, has there been a terrain more suitable for making of pictures or telling stories..." declared William Robinson Leigh, who was to become one of our finest western painters, when he first went west in 1906. Leigh was then forty, but he still found time to get in twenty-five trips to the territory, where he lived with many Indian tribes, as well as with cowboys and, occasionally, horse thieves. The canvas of Grand Canyon at left is considered one of his finest. Charles W. Love, a Denver artist, painted the view of Monument Valley below.

OVERLEAF: *Ferdinand Burgdorff made this study of the Canyon de Chelly, where, centuries before, Indians had discovered a natural fortress in a cave in the face of a cliff and built their adobe homes sixty feet above the canyon floor.*

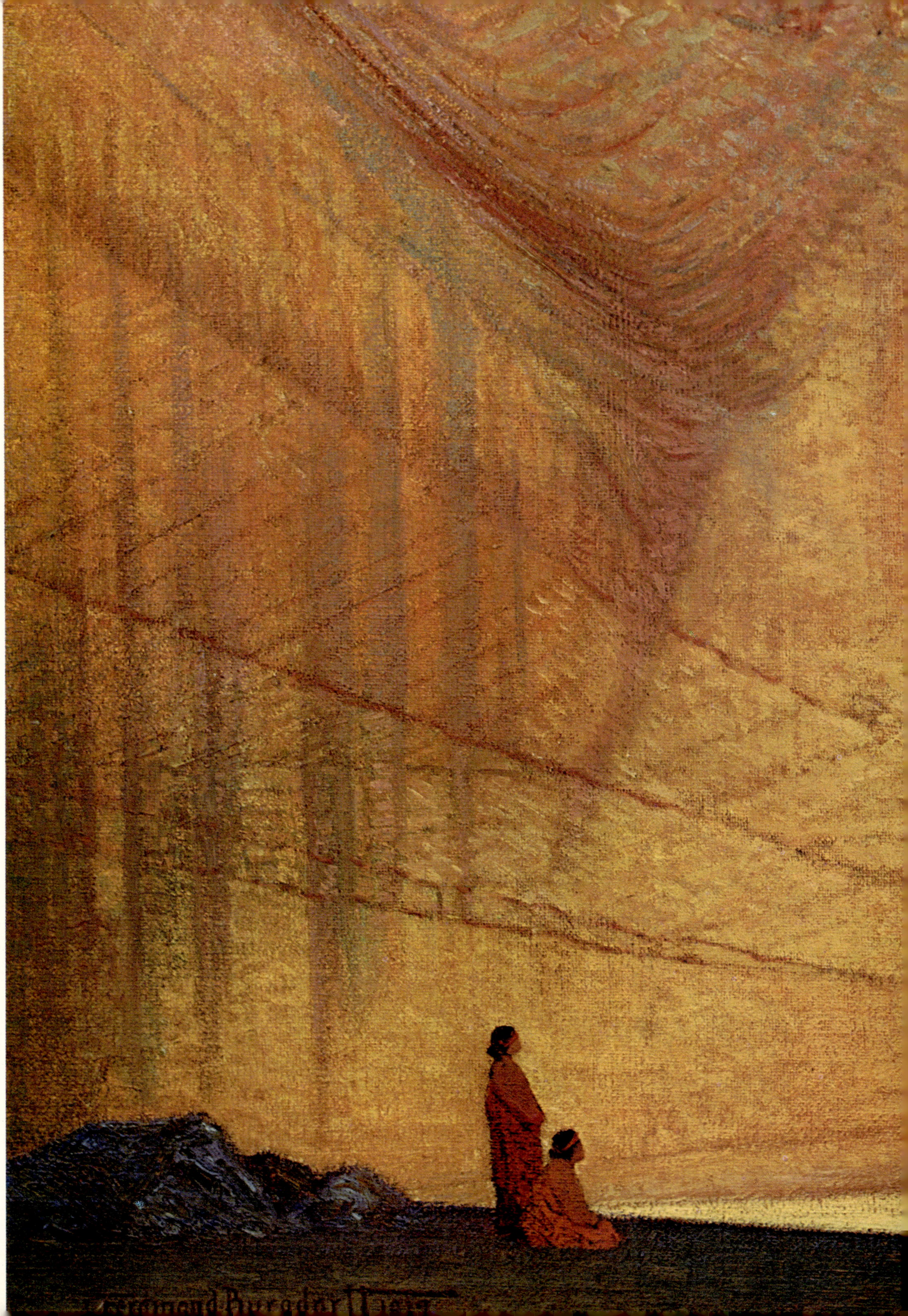

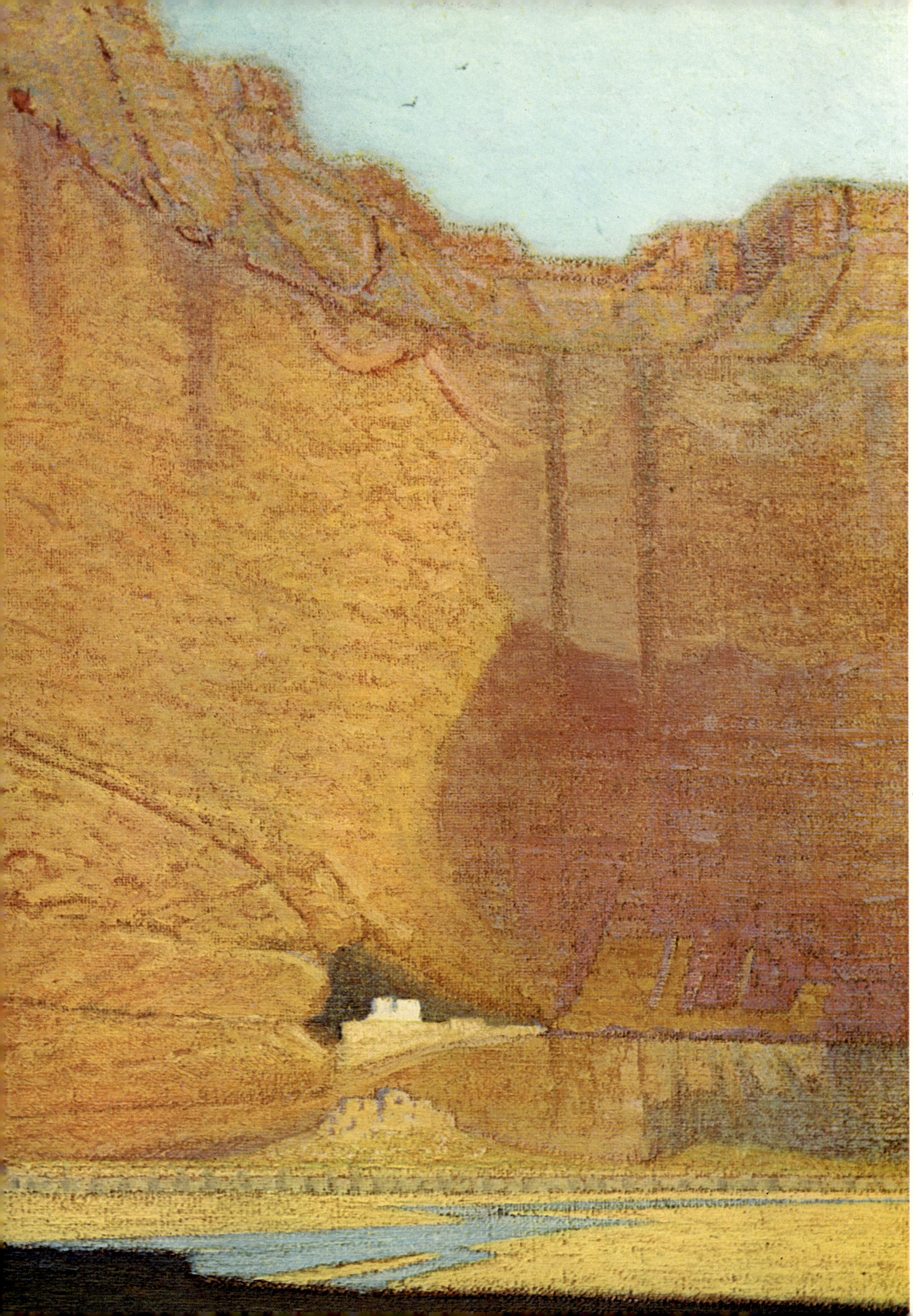

KOYTS-Y-SEE
HOPI

Joseph Henry Sharp was first enthralled by the bright, burnt colors of the Southwest during a visit there in the 1880's. Eventually he settled in Taos, where he devoted himself to painting Indian portraits of such accuracy that his work is useful to modern ethnologists. Below, one of his closely observed subjects broods over a mute memento of the old glories.

Koyts-Y-See, the sober Hopi girl at left, has recently become old enough to wed. This is announced to the Hopi community by her hair, which has been arranged by her mother in the form of the squash blossom, the Hopi symbol of purity. Once married, the young woman will wear her hair in two braids. Edgar Martin Keller painted her portrait.

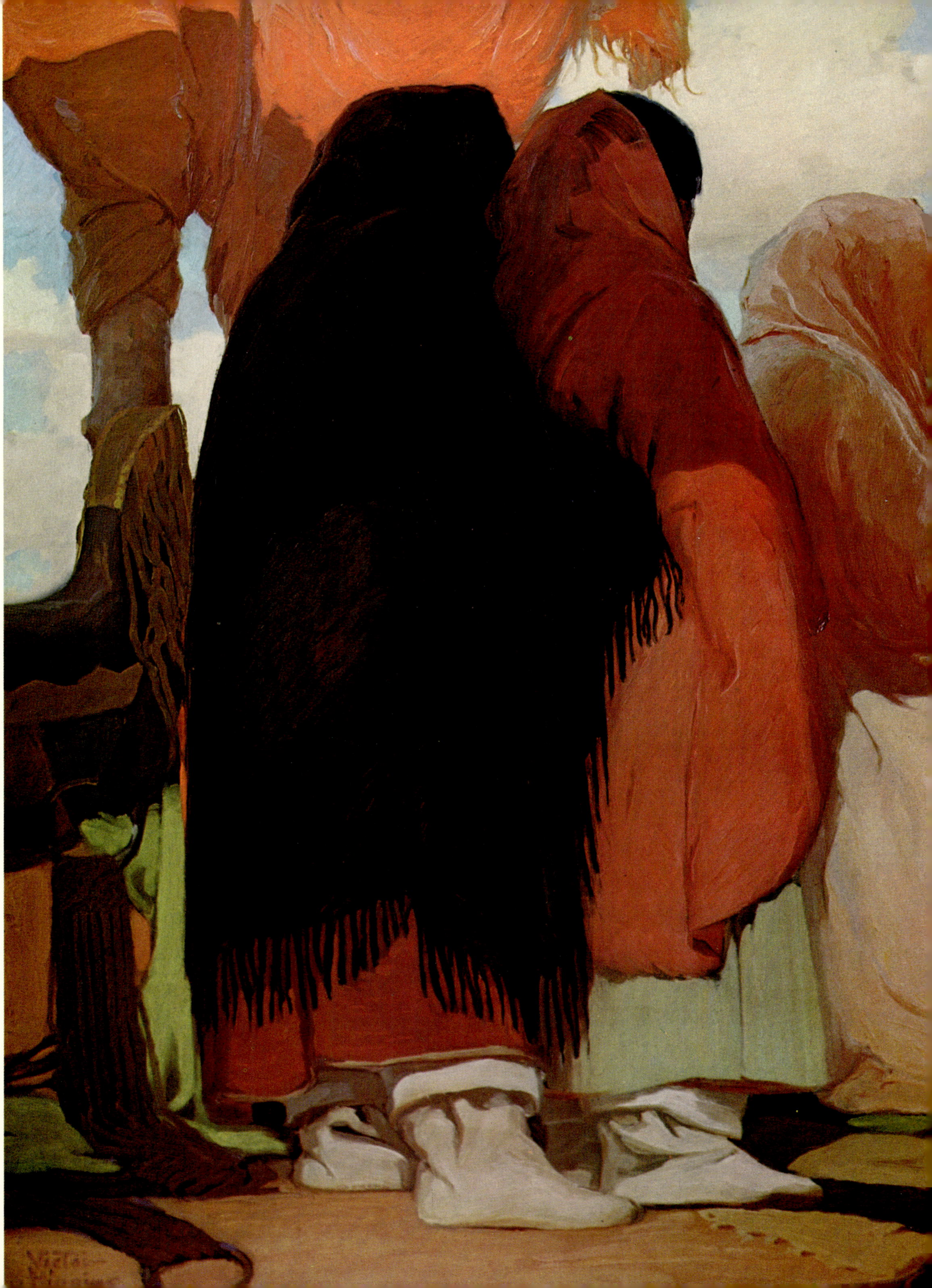

William Victor Higgins, who was more interested in color than in the careful delineation of form, found a perfect subject in the flowing robes of his Three Women of Taos. *The black robe on the woman at left indicates that she is married or aging, a custom of dress absorbed from the Mexicans.*

Many of the Santa Fe artists were fascinated by native rituals. Frederic Kimball Mizen did the study of the sand painters below. These ephemeral paintings were made to cure the sick, petition for blessings, or ward off evil, and had to be destroyed before sunset. Ferdinand Burgdorff's Pueblo Indian stands with ancient patience in the bright sun at right.

66

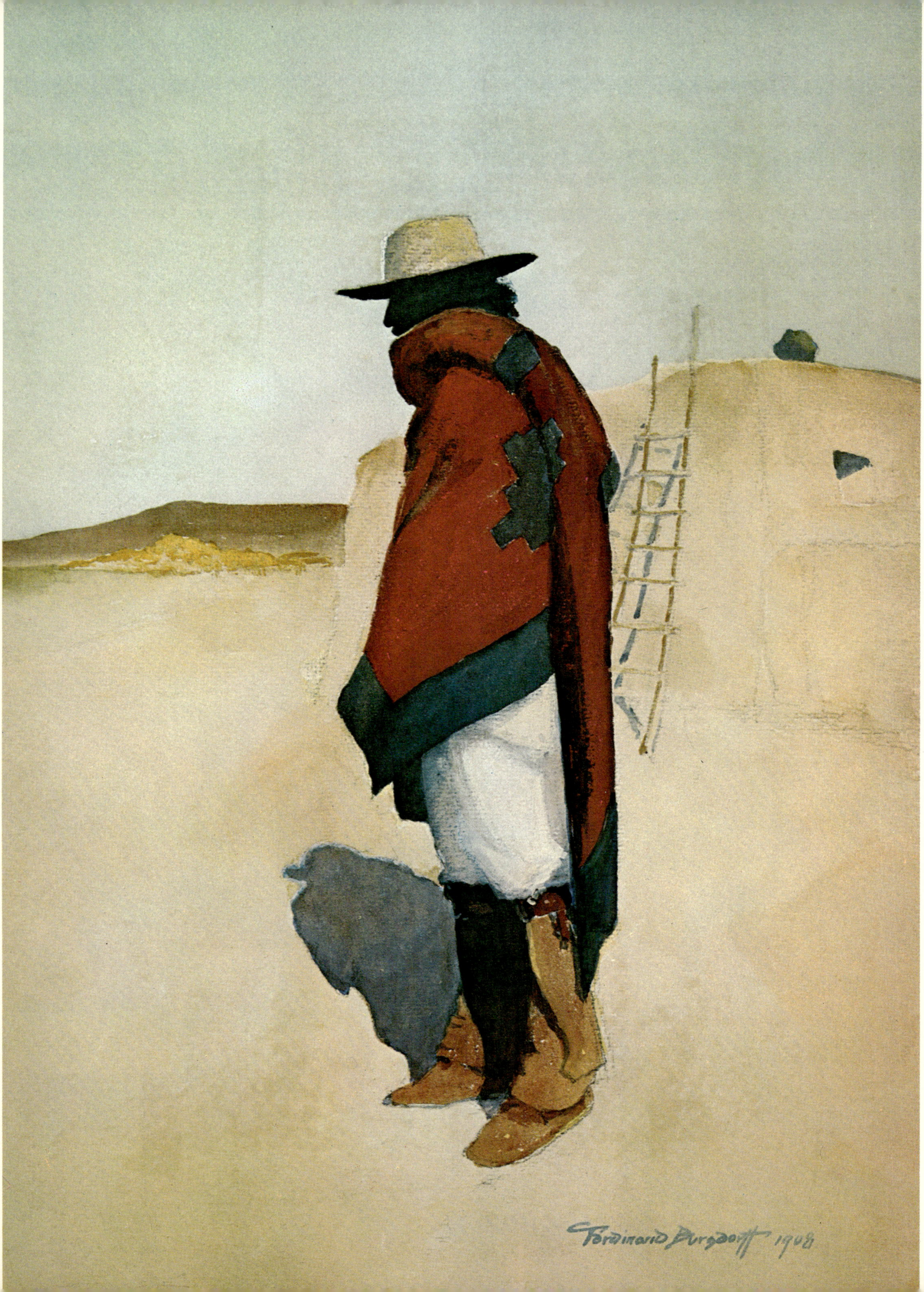
Ferdinand Burgdorff 1908

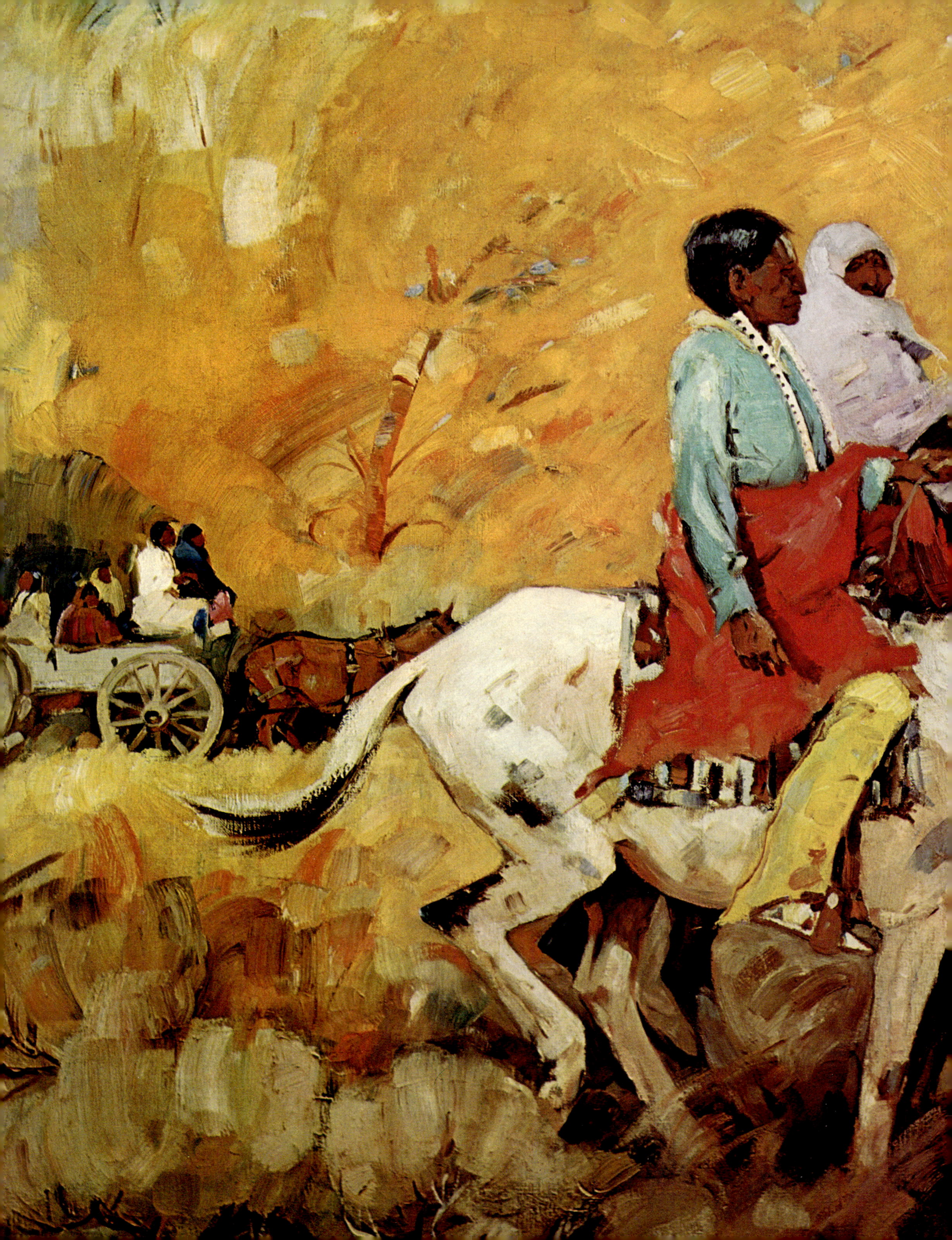

Going to the Pueblo *was painted by LaVerne Nelson Black, who did many vivid studies of Navahos and Apaches while living in Taos and Phoenix.*

This quintessential western scene, with its stagecoach rattling along beneath the huge sky, was the suitable premier acquisition of the Santa Fe Collection. The railroad bought it from the artist, Mrs. Bertha Mengler Dressler, in 1903.

Mario Larrinaga, whose Sky Blue Waters Cumbres Pass *appears above, used his sure grasp of western landscapes in his career as a set designer for Universal Studios in Hollywood and as art director for* RKO *and Warner Brothers.*

This flat, empty place is south of Shiprock in the northwestern corner of New Mexico. The artist, Don Percival, was born in England but moved to the Southwest, where he worked among the Hopis and was admitted to their tribe in 1951.

Matthew B. Ridgway

loads and heavier can be dropped safely.

Since we had no heavy artillery, we had to rely on the support of fighter-bombers, dive bombers. This means that an airborne unit faced almost hopeless odds if it was dropped beyond the range of such aircraft and if it had to face a strong, balanced enemy force supported by armor. And yet time after time in the Italian campaign, plans were drawn up to drop an airborne division or task force far beyond fighter support, or to send out the units piecemeal, or to misuse them as infantry on ground assaults and river crossings—in one case, to drop the division on Capua, a heavily built-up industrial city.

I spent a lot of time and annoyed a good many higher commanders in opposing those foolish schemes.

How best to use the 82nd Airborne Division was a matter of considerable study and planning at Eisenhower's headquarters in Algeria in July and August of 1943. The invasion of the Italian mainland was set for September 9. The Italians had secretly negotiated a surrender. General Eisenhower in Carthage and Field Marshal Pietro Badoglio, who was now the Italian premier, were to make a joint announcement by radio of the Italian surrender on the night of September 8, and early the next morning General Mark Clark was to land at the Gulf of Salerno with the equivalent of four divisions. The Fifth Army would expand the beachhead, drive on to Naples, and then overrun Italy. The 82nd Airborne would be used somewhere, somehow, in that operation.

After a remarkable series of orders, counterorders, plans, and cancellations that had the 82nd in a state of hyperreadiness for combat, Ridgway was called to 15th Army Group headquarters at Siracusa, Sicily, on September 1. He was told that he was now to parachute and airland the strongest possible task forces on or near three airfields immediately west and northwest of Rome on the nights of September 8 and 9. There his mission would be to defend that city in conjunction with Italian forces in the area. He was informed that the high importance of the mission outweighed any objections there might be as to lack of time to properly brief troops or any other serious defects that might arise. The name of the operation was Giant II.

Ridgway was appalled. He knew the difficult mountain terrain that would face ground troops moving north from Salerno to Rome. Everyone knew that the Germans had eighteen good divisions in Italy, six of them near Rome. That city was far beyond fighter-plane support from Sicily. He was convinced that the operation would fail and that his young men would be massacred.

He sat throughout the night of September 3 discussing the operation with General W. Bedell Smith, Eisenhower's chief of staff, and with Italian military representatives. The Italian officers promised to deliver seven hundred trucks and thousands of gallons of fuel to the fields, to have telephones, picks, shovels, wire, and civilian laborers on hand, to clear the Tiber River so that an amphibious task force could land, and to silence the coastal antiaircraft guns over which the transport planes would have to fly. Ridgway read in their faces that they could not fulfill those commitments. In a private talk with Smith he poured out his misgivings; Smith listened sympathetically and arranged for him to meet with Field Marshal Sir Harold Alexander, supreme commander in the Mediterranean.

"I stated my case as earnestly and persuasively as I could," Ridgway says. "I admired General Alexander. He was the last man off the beach at Dunkirk. When I was NATO commander eight years later, we became friends, and once, with a grin, he actually offered to fire my deputy if I wished, the deputy being Field Marshal Montgomery and the offer being one I appreciated but of course declined. But on this occasion Alexander gave me a fast brush-off. He did it in a casual way, scarcely seeming to listen to what I had to say. When he dismissed me, he said: 'Don't give it another thought, Ridgway. Contact will be made with your division in three days. Five days at the most.'"

Ridgway was now in one of the cruelest dilemmas a commander can face. He could conclude that he had done his best and should now obey orders, even though he felt they represented an unreasonable risk and would pointlessly destroy his division as a fighting unit. Or he could persist in his objections, run the risk of censure, and perhaps see his men leave on the suicidal mission without him, under another commander. He discussed the situation with his division artillery commander, Brigadier General Maxwell D. Taylor, who had been with him at the September 1 briefing at Siracusa and at the conference with the Italian officers. They both agreed that more intelligence was essential, and together they went to Bedell Smith with the proposal that a reliable officer be sent secretly into Rome to meet with Premier Badoglio and learn from him whether he could give the essential help that was being promised in his name. Alexander rejected the idea as too risky.

Ridgway ordered his division to prepare for the Rome drop, now only a few days away, but he and Taylor once again went to Smith with a renewed request that some way be found to reconsider the operation. Taylor volunteered to make the secret trip to Rome. Smith went back to Alexander again—this time, Ridgway believes, with some added arguments of his own. Alexander finally agreed to submit the matter to Eisenhower, the supreme commander. Eisenhower decided to send Taylor to Rome on the mission. ("The risks he ran," Eisenhower said later, "were greater than I asked any other agent or emissary to undertake during the war.") With Taylor went William T. Gardiner, a colonel in the Troop Carrier Command, a well-known New England lawyer and a former governor of Maine, who had become interested in flying at age forty-five. If Taylor and Gardiner learned that the airdrop was feasible, they were to stay and arrange for safe delivery of the airfields to the incoming paratroopers. If not, they were to radio back a message in the clear containing the word *innocuous*.

In uniform, carrying musette bags and a radio, they boarded a British PT boat and were taken to the island of Ustica, where they were transferred to an Italian corvette that landed them at Gaeta. In the guise of captured airmen they travelled in a military ambulance some seventy-five miles to Rome. They were shocked at what they learned from Badoglio, General Carboni, and other officers. The Italians had expected a full-scale landing by sea, followed by a massive airdrop. The Germans knew of the planned operation, were reinforcing their units around Rome, and had cut back on supplies of gasoline and ammunition to their Italian allies. The Italian forces could hold back the Germans for no more than twelve hours, after which Rome would be overrun. A landing of an American paratroop force appeared to be suicidal. And Badoglio had now decided not to announce that Italy was signing an armistice.

On various departure fields in Sicily and Tunis the Troop Carrier Wing had its C-47's in formation, and six thousand paratroopers were loading their equipment containers and making a last check on orders, plans, rations, ammunition, and weapons. Ridgway had written his last letters, said his last good-byes, and talked with the division chaplain. He was waiting, playing cribbage with Colonel Ralph P. Eaton, his chief of staff, when, twenty minutes before the first planes were to take off, General Lyman Lemnitzer appeared on the field. Taylor's message had been received; it contained the word *innocuous*; and Lemnitzer, fearing a delay or miscarriage in his radio message, had boarded a plane at Eisenhower's headquarters and brought the information personally. The wing commander was ordered to stand by. Giant II was postponed and then cancelled. The invasion of Salerno, however, took place the next morning as scheduled.

Ridgway has written in his memoirs: "When the time comes that I must meet my Maker, the source of most humble pride to me will [be] . . . the fact that I was guided to make the decision to oppose this thing, at the risk of my career, right up to the top. I deeply and sincerely believe that by taking the stand I took we saved the lives of thousands of brave men."

The 82nd landed at and dropped into the Salerno area on eight hours' notice and, fighting as a light-infantry division, received much of the credit for saving that beachhead. When Naples fell on October 6, Ridgway entered the city with General Clark, standing with him in the turret of an antitank vehicle. Allied ground troops reached Rome, not in five days, but nine months after the cancellation of Giant II.

In England in the spring of 1944, while planning and training for the invasion of Normandy, Ridgway fought as hard to have his division used as he had earlier fought against its misuse. (His 504th Parachute Regiment had been held in Italy to fight at Anzio, which caused no little confusion in the German intelligence offices.) Plans called for sending in seventeen thousand airborne troops on D-day—the 101st under Taylor to drop near Carentan, the 82nd under Ridgway to drop near Ste. Mère-Église, eight miles inland from Utah Beach. The British Air Chief Marshal, Sir Trafford Leigh-Mallory, opposed the American drop as too dangerous. He told Montgomery, Bradley, and Eisenhower that the C-47's, flying in at six hundred feet, would be shot down by German ground fire. Loss in paratrooper strength, he believed, would be not less than 50 per cent before the gliders came in at dawn, and some 70 per cent of the gliders would be shot out of the air or would crash on the Normandy hedgerows. Ridgway, speaking as the senior American Airborne general, insisted that the losses, though certain to be heavy, would be acceptable in relation to the importance of the mission and to the chance of success. Eisenhower ordered that the plan hold firm.

Ridgway and his staff had rewritten their manuals after the Sicily and Italian mainland operations. Everything possible, including most "comfort" items, should be eliminated in favor of a heavier man-load of ammunition, grenades, and bazookas. A drop of "pathfinders" should precede the main drop to mark landing zones with lights and radar beams.

The 82nd's six thousand paratroopers took off in a great sky train beginning at 10 P.M. on June 5, Ridgway going in with the 2nd Battalion of his 505th Parachute Regiment. His division was to land in and around an area containing Neuville-au-Plain, Ste. Mère-Église, Chef du Pont, Étienville, and Amfreville. It was to capture and hold the causeways—the elevated roadways—running inland across the flooded areas behind Utah Beach, thus permitting expansion of the beachhead to the south and west. It was to destroy the crossings of the Douve River. It was then to be prepared to advance to the west as ordered by corps headquarters.

"I landed in a field," Ridgway says, "and worked my way out of my chute. In doing that I dropped my automatic pistol. I groped around in the high grass, found it, and began crawling toward the nearest hedge. I saw a dark standing figure, but before I could challenge it, I saw it move and realized it was a cow. That gave my spirits a lift, because I knew the field wasn't mined or there wouldn't be a cow wandering around in it. On the other side of the hedge I gave a challenge and got back the proper response. It was Captain Willard Follmer, the first man I had met when I went inland in Sicily. He was sitting then against a tree, with a broken ankle. Now he was sitting against a tree, with a back sprain that rendered him immobile."

By daybreak Ridgway had rounded up a few of his command group and established a division headquarters in an orchard just west of Ste. Mère-Église. Some 50 gliders came in at first light with headquarters elements, jeeps, and 57-mm antitank guns, each carrying about 3,750 pounds and landing at about 60 miles per hour. Colonel Eaton was injured in a crash and was out of action. Some 375 more gliders came in the next day with two airborne artillery battalions, 105-mm short-barrel howitzers, and 4,000 more airborne infantrymen.

The division took Ste. Mère-Église, the first French town to be liberated; Lieutenant Colonel Edward Krause raised over it an American flag that had flown over Naples. At dawn on the third day contact was made with a patrol of the 4th Division, which had landed on Utah Beach and fought its way inland. Ridgway later learned that his division had landed on top of and destroyed the 91st German Division, which had moved into the area two weeks earlier. Most of his men had dropped or landed in an area five by seven miles in size. Some fifty planeloads had been widely dispersed, but the troopers cut all enemy communications lines as they worked their way back across country to assemble. Acting now as ground troops, the division captured St.-Sauveur-le-Vicomte and then fought to the edge of La Haye-du-Puits, where it was relieved on July 8. It had been engaged for thirty-three days without relief or replacements and had carried out all its D-day missions except that of crossing the Merderet River, one bank of which it had seized on D-plus-3. Losses were high but far below those feared by Leigh-Mallory (who apologized handsomely to Eisenhower for having burdened him with a wrong prediction). Twelve hundred and eighty-two men were killed, 2,373 seriously wounded—46 out of every 100 men. The toll was higher among unit leaders. "We lost and had to replace fourteen infantry battalion commanders from within their units," Ridgway says. "Considering we went into battle with twelve, that was a tremendous loss."

The 82nd returned to the Midlands in England in July, where it received a hero's welcome from the English. Ridgway, following the events in France through that summer, regretted that so much time had been devoted at command conferences to alternative plans in case of failure, while almost none had been spent on what courses to follow to exploit unexpected successes. "We were as unprepared to capitalize on the unexpected breakout at St. Lô," he says, "as the Austrians and Germans had been at Caporetto in the fall of 1917."

In August he turned over the 82nd to General James M. Gavin and took command of the XVIII Airborne Corps. At one time or another during the remainder of the war in Europe twenty-two divisions were under his corps' command. In September, Gavin's 82nd and Taylor's 101st were lent to the British for fifty-eight days in the line, in the airdrop around Eindhoven-Nijmegen. This, Operation Market Garden, was Montgomery's ill-fated attempt to trap a German army in Holland, with its back to the sea. Ridgway flew, drove, and walked (without command responsibility) to visit the command posts of his two American divisions. When he found he could walk a mile and a half up a road that an advance element of British armor was unwilling to try, he concluded that stronger leadership from the top command could have brought British ground forces into contact with the 1st British Airborne Division, which had been dropped beyond the Rhine. He is pleased that, with the popularity of Cornelius Ryan's *A Bridge Too Far*, the world now recognizes the outstanding performance of the two American airborne divisions in Market Garden and no longer thinks of it as solely a British operation.

Eisenhower released the XVIII Corps from theater reserve on December 18, and Ridgway commanded it through the six weeks of the Battle of the Bulge. On Sunday, March 11, he, Gavin, and Taylor flew to Rheims for a conference with Eisenhower at SHAEF forward headquarters. ("They all looked superbly fit and keen in every way," Captain Harry C. Butcher wrote in his diary that night.) During dinner Eisenhower took a telephone call from Omar Bradley, who informed him that one of Courtney Hodges' units had captured an intact bridge across the Rhine, at the town of Remagen.

Ridgway participated in the last major airdrop of the war thirteen days later, when an American and a British division under his command were put down across the Rhine at Wesel in support of the XII Corps of the British Army. He crossed the river in an Alligator, an amphibious tracked vehicle, and in a fire fight with a German patrol that night received a nonincapacitating wound from a grenade splinter that he still carries in his right shoulder. In April he led four divisions in an eight-day drive that cleaned out the Ruhr pocket. When he was two miles from Field Marshal Walther von Model's headquarters, he sent one of his aides, Captain Frank Brandstetter, with a flag of truce to say that in order to save lives he would accept the Germans' surrender. The aide came back with a German staff officer who conveyed Model's refusal on the ground of personal honor. Ridgway wrote a second letter, in which he invoked the name of Robert E. Lee, who was a man of honor and had surrendered his armies eighty years ago that month ("I remembered the date from a lecture I had heard by Douglas Freeman"). Model sent back another refusal, this time by his chief of staff, Colonel Fritz Schultz-Madler, who had advised Model to surrender and who accepted Ridgway's invitation to become a pris-

As supreme commander in the Far East, Ridgway happily greets his wife and his young son Matty at a Tokyo airport on May 10, 1951.
COLLECTION OF MATTHEW B. RIDGWAY

oner of war. Model had publicly criticized Field Marshal von Paulus for surrendering at Stalingrad; now he chose to walk into the forest near Düsseldorf and shoot himself. Ridgway offered the field marshal's handsome Mercedes-Benz staff car to General Bradley, who politely declined it. The front moved forward, and Ridgway never knew who ended up with the car.

In the last weeks of the war in Europe he led four divisions—three American and one British—in support of the British Second Army's drive to the Baltic to cut off the Danish peninsula and save it from Soviet occupation. In less than one week his corps moved by truck and jeep nearly three hundred miles, from the Ruhr to the Elbe, across that river on a pontoon bridge, and sixty miles eastward to meet the Russians. In setting up a thirty-mile buffer zone with the Russians he found them at the first meeting to be somewhat stubborn and suspicious, though they made no real difficulties. General Andrei Smirnov, his opposite number, a corps commander and a hero of the Soviet Union, he found to be much more agreeable on a second meeting, and with him he achieved a cautious but pleasant relationship. (Almost a year later Ridgway was on his way from Caserta, his headquarters as commander of the Mediterranean Theater, to a new post in London as representative of General Eisenhower, the army chief of staff, to the Military Staff Committee of the United Nations. Going by way of Berlin, he decided to call on General Smirnov, who was then Russian military commander in the city, and found him an entirely different person: stiff, unreceptive, cold as ice. Twenty-eight years later, in the fall of 1973, Ridgway received a telephone call at his Pittsburgh home from a G-2 officer in Washington. General Smirnov, the officer said, had visited the American embassy in Moscow and wished to send his warm greetings and best wishes for good health to General Ridgway. Did General Ridgway wish to answer the communication? He responded with cordial wishes for General Smirnov's good health and happiness in his retirement. "I would be happy to meet him again," he says today.)

In August, 1945, Ridgway started for the Far East, where he was to assume command of all airborne operations in the planned invasion of the Japanese mainland. He was over San Francisco Bay when the pilot informed his passengers that news of the Japanese surrender had just been received.

When Ridgway returned from Japan early in 1946, he found that his earlier marriage could no longer survive the long period of separation and that divorce was the only solution. While serving as chairman of the Inter-American Defense Board in Washington, he met Mary "Penny" Anthony, secretary to the United States Navy delegate on the board. She was still in her twenties; a correspondent for *Collier's* described her as "a strikingly beautiful woman who makes other women reach uneasily for their mirrors." They were married in December, 1947. A son, Matthew B. Ridgway, Jr. ("Matty"), was born in 1949 while Ridgway was commander in chief of the Caribbean command.

"Penny has played an indispensable role in my career," Ridgway says. "It was not an easy assignment for a young wife, especially at first, before people came to know her. I was a three-star general and the senior officer, or commander, or both, at the posts where I was stationed. This meant that she was the General's Lady, the 'First Lady' on the post. Human nature being what it is, she naturally was subject to the envy of those loyal army wives who felt that their husbands should be in the top position. Penny ignored the petty annoyances. Her common sense, tact, and thoughtfulness for others won over everyone with whom she came in contact." Other witnesses have agreed, including General Marshall, who said, "She amazes me. Her poise in a job like this is truly remarkable."

Through five postwar years on his various military and diplomatic assignments Ridgway was horrified to watch the headlong rush of the American people and Congress to cut back their armed forces and dismantle their arms industry—a development, he feels, that General Eisenhower, as army chief of staff, seemed to endorse or at least to accept without noticeable public protest. In October, 1949, he became General J. Lawton Collins' deputy chief of staff for administration and training, and he took up residence at Quarters Seven at Fort Myer. He personally pushed development of the new 3.5-inch bazooka, the airdrop of heavier weapons and vehicles, and the 105-mm recoilless cannon, a light, highly mobile artillery piece. And he wrestled with curtailed programs and reduced budgets imposed under Secretary of War Louis Johnson's policy of "trimming off the fat." His forebodings were realized in June, 1950, when the North Koreans crossed the 38th parallel in a massive invasion of South Korea. Throughout the summer he studied the daily reports of poorly equipped, undertrained skeleton army regiments sent to fight in Korea, where they were mauled, decimated, and driven back, first by the North Koreans and then by Chinese troops in overwhelmingly superior numbers. "If we had had properly armed and trained units in 1950," Ridgway says, "properly deployed, we could have choked off that aggression in a relatively short time with much less loss of life." Ridgway became, in effect, the Army's operations officer for Korea, and though he did not know it, he had been tapped by the chiefs of staff to assume command of the Eighth Army in the event of an emergency.

In early August, President Truman sent Averell Harriman to the Far East to meet with General MacArthur and convey to him the President's policies. Generals Ridgway and Lauris Norstad were directed to accompany Harriman. Ridgway had known MacArthur since the early 1920's, when he was a faculty member and MacArthur was superintendent at West Point. He respected the general's personal courage, quick mind, and tactical brilliance, his qualities of leadership, and his record as a soldier-statesman in the occupation of Japan. But he was profoundly disturbed by his conduct of operations in the Korean War. "He was trying to command General Walton

Walker and the Eighth Army from Tokyo," Ridgway says, seven hundred miles from the battlefields. He dispersed his forces recklessly in his headlong dash north to the border of Manchuria and the Soviet Union, and he misread his intelligence reports when he asserted in the fall of 1950 that the war would be "over in two weeks" and that "the Chinese are not coming into this war." He persisted for some days in refusing to believe that China had entered the war, even after it was painfully evident that they had entered it in massive numbers. He deliberately disobeyed a specific directive from the Joint Chiefs when he placed non-Korean troops in northern provinces bordering Manchuria and the Soviet Union. His reports to the Joint Chiefs, which came across my desk, began to swing from one extreme to the other: things were good, things were bad, the war would be won, the positions in Korea could not be held.

Any military commander is human and may make mistakes. When he does, it's part of his job as a soldier to accept responsibility for what he has done and to find out why it went wrong. MacArthur refused to do this in Korea, and when his blunders resulted in smashing reversals, he called for a broadening of the war—an air attack to demolish the air bases and industry of Manchuria, a blockade of the seacoast of China and destruction of its industrial centers, and use of Nationalist Chinese troops in Formosa to fight in Korea. At that time we had only two battle-ready divisions in the Continental United States, one Army, one Marine.

In effect, MacArthur was attempting to change and guide the stated policies of the government. In doing this he was challenging civilian control of the military arm as established by law and tradition, and in my opinion he came perilously close to insubordination.

Ridgway and his wife were spending the evening of December 22, 1950, at the home of a next-door neighbor in Fort Myer when, shortly before midnight, he received a telephone call from General Collins, army chief of staff. Collins said: "Matt, I'm sorry to have to tell you that Johnny Walker has been killed in a jeep accident. You have been designated to take over. I want you to get your things together and get out there just as soon as you can." Next morning, over coffee in their second-floor study, Ridgway said as gently as he could: "Penny, I've got something to tell you. I'm going to Korea to replace Johnny Walker, who's been killed in an accident."

At his briefing Collins asked him what officers he wished to take with him on the trip. He replied: "I'll go this one alone. It's Christmas, and even a bachelor will have made plans." He remade his will, bought some heavy underwear, and had a short, premature Christmas party with his wife and son. He arrived in Tokyo, alone, just before midnight on Christmas Day. He discussed the situation with MacArthur, who gave him a free hand, and flew to Korea the next day.

He found, as he expected, that he was in command of a shattered army. It had conducted itself bravely in withdrawing before an attack by superior numbers, and it had lost little of its heavy weapons and equipment; but now it had only three of its seven U.S. divisions in the battle zone, and these were badly depleted. The men were tired and dispirited, they lacked confidence in themselves and their leaders, and they were subject to what had become known as "bugout fever." The Joint Chiefs had drawn up contingency plans for evacuating the peninsula. Some observers, indeed, assumed that Ridgway had been appointed receiver in bankruptcy.

Instead he undertook measures to give the army new life, purpose, and fighting spirit before the next Chinese attack, which was expected on New Year's Eve, five days away. He visited the command posts of the three American divisions, of the two American corps, and of South Korean divisions and corps, assessing the morale of men and officers. He told his commanders to ignore previous orders to hold their positions "at all costs": they were to give ground where absolutely necessary but to withdraw fighting, in a coordinated and orderly manner, on predetermined phase lines, inflicting maximum damage on the enemy. No unit was to be left to be overwhelmed and destroyed, and units that were cut off were to be fought for and brought back unless a major commander, after personal appraisal on the spot, decided that their relief would result in the loss of equal or greater numbers ("I knew it was vital, in restoring the fighting spirit of the troops, to make clear to all of them that their leaders were concerned for their safety and would not expend their lives needlessly"). At his request South Korean President Syngman Rhee put tens of thousands of laborers to digging trenches and gun emplacements in rearward lines.

Ridgway ordered commanders to get their men off the roads and onto the high ground ("They were road-bound") and to increase their patrolling. He asked that exhausted field commanders be returned to the United States without prejudice and be replaced with fresh officers. He moved up the army forward-command post. After listening to the gripes of the men in the field he ordered the kitchens to move closer to the front lines and to provide large amounts of hot food, with hot meat served at least seven times out of every ten days. He had helicopters carry in writing paper, envelopes that did not stick together, warm clothing, and great bundles of gloves ("I knew from personal experience how easy it is to leave a glove behind or to drop it to fire a weapon and then not see it again"). He stopped the indoctrination talks on the noble aims and righteous cause of the United Nations and replaced them with sterner stuff ("I treated them as disciplined, trained men who would take professional pride in their toughness and skill as fighters and who wanted to win").

He flew everywhere in a light liaison plane or a helicopter and day after day appeared in forward positions, always in an open jeep. A Turkish commander told a *New York Times* correspondent: "Ridgway is here almost every day. He makes our morale boost." He was everywhere recognizable for his dress: pile cap with the bill tied back, blue and white Airborne patch on his shoulder, jump boots, and a parachutist's web harness. To the harness were taped the parachutist's first-aid kit and a live hand grenade. He has insisted for twenty-five years, sincerely but without much success, that in carrying the grenade he had no intention of emulating the showmanship of Patton with his pearl-handled pistols, MacArthur with his battered braided hat and underslung corncob pipe, Montgomery with his beret, Wingate with his beard and pith helmet. "I wore it solely for self-preservation," he says. "It might have been very useful if my plane had gone down in enemy territory." Whatever the intent, he achieved instant identification and a reputation for audacity, and his men gave him the ultimate compliment of an admiring nickname, "Old Iron Tit."

The Communists began their assault on schedule on New Year's Eve. The Eighth Army gave up Seoul for the second time in the war. Still fighting and in close contact with the enemy, it withdrew some seventy-five miles and then stood firm. On January 25, 1951, one month after his arrival in the Far East, Ridgway ordered a general counterattack with two army corps, about 365,000 men. By February 9 his troops were back to the Han River, driving before them a force about three times their size. James Michener, writing a profile on Ridgway for *Life* magazine early in 1952, said: "Within a few electrifying weeks Matt Ridgway had all his officers working on plans for attack, in a change of spirit and purpose so swift that none would have believed it possible. . . . In Korea the man has become enveloped in a great legend—a legend vastly complimentary and almost wholly true."

The enemy twice renewed its attack, using massed forces for the first time in the war, suffered heavy losses, and was halted. Ridgway organized a February offensive. The Eighth Army retook Seoul, drove across the 38th parallel with relatively low losses, and halted. General Collins wrote in his book on the Korean War: ". . . no longer was there much talk of evacuation. General Ridgway . . . was responsible for this dramatic change." The military historian S. L. A. Marshall calls it "the most dramatic American command achievement of this century." Ridgway gave the credit to his men. "The American flag never flew over a prouder, tougher, more spirited and more competent fighting force," he said in 1967.

On March 24 General MacArthur precipitated a showdown between himself and the Joint Chiefs of Staff, with whom he had been feuding, and between himself and President Truman. On April 11 Truman relieved him of his command and appointed Ridgway his successor. Ridgway heard the news in a hail and snow storm on the line in Korea. He flew to Tokyo the next day. General Collins has recorded that one of Ridgway's first acts as supreme commander in the Far East was to have his chief of staff catalogue all orders, directives, and restrictions received by MacArthur since the start of the war.

Ridgway now carried on four jobs from his office in the Dai Ichi Building. He was deputy for the seventeen members of the United Nations furnishing troops for the continuing war in Korea. He was commander of all the United States forces in the Far East. He represented the eleven Allied Powers of World War II as military governor of Japan. And he was director of United Nations negotiations for a truce in Korea.

In June, 1951, the Chinese dropped their talk about the "inevitability" of Communist victory and let it be known that they were disposed to begin negotiations for a truce; discreet inquiries in Moscow confirmed that the offer was genuine. Ridgway (now wearing a fourth star), on authorization from Washington, broadcast an invitation to the Communists to meet with U.N. delegates, and a few days later the first meeting of two years of painful, crisis-filled negotiations began at Kaesong (briefly) and then continued at Panmunjom.

Mrs. Ridgway and Matty joined him in Tokyo in May, 1951, after a separation of five months—a time she describes as the unhappiest of her life. Ridgway, frequently absent on trips to Korea, relied heavily on his wife to fulfill social obligations that were a part of his work, and he declared near the end of his stay in the Far East: "If I have had any success with the Japanese, it is due to my wife." She represented him at the funeral of the dowager empress, and she accompanied him to a precedent-breaking luncheon in the Japanese Imperial Palace as guests of Emperor Hirohito and Empress Nagako. It was the first visit of a supreme commander to the Imperial Palace.

Ridgway returned to the United States in May, 1952, on his way to a new assignment in Europe. A private talk with Commander in Chief Harry Truman began a whirlwind week. He, Mrs. Ridgway, and three-year-old Matty then rode on the President's private train to attend a 150th anniversary ceremony at West Point, where Ridgway received a second oak leaf cluster for his Distinguished Service Medal, pinned on his tunic by President Truman for "magnificent personal leadership" in the Korean War. Back in Washington he testified at length on the Far East behind closed doors before the Senate Armed Services Committee. He went to Fort McNair for a special review and reception. He addressed a joint session of the U.S. Congress and a joint session of Washington's three top press clubs. And for his new job he bought a tailor-made full-dress military-diplomatic uniform. The swallowtail black suit had epaulets, gold braid around the sleeves, and gold braid down the seams of the trousers.

The new job was that of supreme commander of NATO forces in Europe, succeeding General Eisenhower. There were problems. The time had come for the NATO commander to divest himself of political activities and get about the business of procuring weapons and organizing a military force. And, as one columnist put it, Eisenhower had distributed the pledges at a giant bond rally; now it was up to Ridgway to collect on them—in a declining market.

The Ridgways lived in Villa St. Pierre near Paris, in the town of Marne-la-Coquette. The general was away much of the time on visits to one or another of the fourteen NATO nations; when she did not accompany him, Mrs. Ridgway visited art galleries, attended the opera, painted landscapes (one of her hobbies), and organized American army wives in Paris for duty in military hospitals in and around the city. During the thirteen-month stay in Europe young Matty, by all accounts and appearances a delightful child, was one of the world's most photographed persons: standing at salute beside his father, mowing down honor guards with his toy gun, entering or leaving airplanes with his doting parents. When the Ridgways were presented to the British royal family at Buckingham Palace, Queen Elizabeth asked Mrs. Ridgway: "How is little Matty? I've seen so many pictures of him that I feel as if I know him."

Ridgway had twelve battle-worthy divisions when he took over the NATO command in June, 1952. At the end of his tour of duty he had some eighty divisions, active and reserve, in varying stages of strength and readiness—still far fewer than he felt were necessary to protect western Europe on a four-thousand-mile frontier against a possible enemy that had a hundred and twenty-five divisions, exclusive of satellite forces. On leaving Europe, Ridgway was expected to write farewell letters to appropriate personages in each NATO country, to be sent in diplomatic pouches or delivered by proxy by his aides. Instead he made a round of personal courtesy calls in each of the fourteen capitals.

He returned to the United States to become army chief of staff and on October 1, 1953, moved into that mecca of ambitious army officers, Quarters One at Fort Myer. The neighbors soon became accustomed to two sights: the general walking the two-odd miles to and from the Pentagon and the general standing on the front porch each evening with Matty, both saluting the lowering of the flag at retreat. He and Mrs. Ridgway asked General and Mrs. Marshall to accept a key to their old home and to use a second-floor suite whenever they wished to spend time in Washington; they did stay there several times.

Ridgway had now reached the highest post in his profession, but his two-year term was to be one of frustration and anguish of spirit. This was the period when Senator Joseph McCarthy was running rampant and Secretary of the Army Robert Stevens was being brutalized by attacks on himself and some of his officers. Of those attacks Theodore H. White wrote on March 30, 1954:

> If morale in the officer corps at the Pentagon is still good . . . as contrasted with the spirit of the already demoralized State Department, it is because the top men have remained firm. What leadership the Army has received in the past few weeks is ascribed by its officer corps chiefly to Matthew B. Ridgway, its Chief of Staff. Ridgway . . . has kept his silence. But [he] has, almost alone, kept the Army stiff in its dignity without yielding to the temptation to strike back or furnishing the burnt offerings required by the Senator's ambition. The cold Ridgway aloofness to politics . . . has served the Army well.

Another of his problems was an unpleasant relationship with Secretary of Defense Charles Wilson. He admired and got along well both with Wilson's predecessor, Robert A. Lovett, and with Wilson's deputy, Robert Anderson. As army representative on the Joint Chiefs of Staff he respected his fellow professionals, Admiral Carney, Air Force General Twining, and Admiral Radford, chairman, though he was sometimes inclined to agree with the navy man who remarked that Radford acted as if he were still commander of the Pacific Fleet instead of first among equals on a strategic planning staff. But with Mr. Wilson he found no basis for liking and little for respect beyond that officially owed to the civilian head of the military services. Ridgway feels that Wilson came from General Motors to Eisenhower's Cabinet with a firm preconception that something was terribly wrong with the armed forces, particularly the Army, and that, whatever it might be, he would have to take steps to straighten it out. His attitude was reflected in his treatment of those under his authority, including the four service chiefs, whom he often addressed as "you men" and dismissed at meetings with the command to carry out orders as instructed. Wilson was given to long, rambling discussions that had little or nothing to do with the subject of the meeting and was disinclined to inform his military subordinates of the subject in advance, which could mean a series of questions for which no hard, up-to-date information had been gathered. In discussions and briefings he was, Ridgway says, often rudely inattentive, drumming his fingers on the table, gazing out the window at the Washington prospect, and ignoring the views a speaker was presenting.

The relationship was exacerbated by the fact that Wilson was under instruction to cut the military budget and that more than three fourths of the cuts were directed at the Army. Ridgway was asked to reduce his troop strength from 1,500,000 to 1,000,000 by the summer of 1956 and to cut army expenditures from $16.2 billion to $8.9 billion. "Wilson's facile slogan, 'More bang for a buck,'" he says, "sounded very much the same to me as Louis Johnson's 'trimming off the fat.' In Secretary of State Dulles' policy of containment we were offering military aid, alliances, and territorial guarantees to some forty nations ringing the globe. Our foreign commitments were going up, and our Army was going down. The country was beginning to be dangerously overextended."

The cuts were ordered, and the commitments were made under what was called a New Look in military preparedness. Dulles described it in a famous sentence in January, 1954. The United States, he said, intended "to depend principally upon a great capacity to retaliate instantly by means and at places of our own choosing." It was understood that he was referring to the use of atomic weapons.

Ridgway challenged that policy. He believed that to

In his articles, books, speeches, and interviews General Ridgway has expressed only a secondary interest in the fact, the decision, and the act. He has placed greater emphasis on the reasoning, or the philosophy, that leads to action. He has placed primary emphasis on the need to project that reasoning into the future. He has hoped that such projection might serve as a guide in deciding for or against comparable action in similar situations and might benefit those who may be charged with responsibilities comparable to those he carried. His thirty-eight years of experience as a soldier and twenty more as a civilian observer have led him to these basic conclusions:

1. The United States cannot reorder the world. We cannot impose a Pax Americana on other nations. We must recognize the limitations of our national power.

2. War is the ultimate tragedy of mankind. It is a ghastly, wasteful business that settles nothing unless the cause is right and the political objectives are clear-cut and limited.

3. Unlimited military effort—"total war"—would now mean turning the clock back several thousand years.

4. The United States should categorically reject "preventive" war employing nuclear weapons. The use of such weapons would be a deliberate move down the road of international immorality past the point of no return.

5. A precept of Clausewitz has momentous validity today: "The most important single judgment a political or military leader can make is to forecast correctly the nature of the war upon which the nation is to embark. On this everything else depends."

6. We should reject any political involvement that might gradually commit us to military efforts that would jeopardize our basic security and those vital American interests that cannot be compromised. We should ask ourselves: What are the basic purposes behind our major policy decisions? What do we seek to accomplish? Are those purposes and objectives clearly within the scope of our vital national interests? Are we in danger of squandering our resources on a nonvital secondary objective? In the field of foreign relations each and every one of our major political objectives should be seen to lie within the zone of our vital interests, and in each the military objectives should be in conformity with and subordinate to the political objectives.

7. Civilian control of the military establishment is fundamental and unchallengeable in our society and must remain so.

8. Civilian authorities must scrupulously respect the integrity and intellectual honesty of the officer corps. If the military adviser's unrestricted advice is solicited, he should give a fearless and forthright expression of honest, objective, professional opinion. He should neither be expected nor required to give public endorsement to courses of military action against which he has previously recommended. Once the decision has been made and announced by proper civilian authorities, he should give his full support to its execution. He should not be blamed for policy decisions made not by the military but by duly elected or lawfully appointed civilian authorities acting in accord with our constitutional procedures.

9. Our planners must not ignore the moral factor when they consider the use of the immense destructive capability that now exists.

place primary reliance on atomic weapons was to put foreign policy in a strait jacket. It was quite possible, he said, that in any future war there would be a "common refusal" to use atomic weapons, including battlefield tactical bombs and shells. To depend on nuclear weapons would leave the United States incapable of dealing with emergency situations by more conventional means.

He was convinced, moreover, that massive retaliation by means and at places of our own choosing was morally as well as militarily wrong. "It is repugnant to the ideals of a Christian nation," he said. "It is not compatible with what should be the basic aim of the United States in war, which is to win a just and durable peace."

Ridgway opposed the new U.S. defense policy when he was called upon to testify before the Senate Military Appropriations Committee, which did not put him in the odor of sanctity with Secretary Wilson or President Eisenhower. Nor was it any recommendation that Adlai Stevenson and Senator Wayne Morse upheld his views. The President did not like "split papers" from his Joint Chiefs of Staff. General Ridgway's "responsibility for national defense," he said in pure Eisenhowerese, "is, you might say, a special one, or, in a sense, parochial." This evidently was meant to explain Ridgway's recalcitrance, and Wilson remarked to the press in the same vein that he was "a sincere and dedicated general who believes very strongly in the Army." Ridgway was thus astonished at last to hear over the radio the President's statement that the 1955 military program had been "unanimously recommended" by the Joint Chiefs.

A problem arose in the spring of 1954 that was more serious than the conflicts with Senator McCarthy and Secretary Wilson and cuts in army manpower. It was a growing movement, led by important persons in and out of government, to send U.S. military forces to the aid of the French in Indochina. France had suffered more than 170,000 casualties there in its professional army (it sent no conscripts); it had spent nearly $7.5 billion, plus another $4 billion in U.S. aid; and now it had an army trapped at Dien Bien Phu. It asked for U.S. military help, and it indicated that in return it would end its opposition to a main plank in U.S. foreign policy: bringing West Germany into NATO. Secretary Dulles and Admiral Radford, proponents of intervention, held that air and naval action alone would save Indochina, with a massive air strike if necessary, using not more than two atomic bombs. Ground troops would not be needed.

To Ridgway this was the 1944 Rome airdrop all over again, but now multiplied thousands of times in its consequences. He opposed intervention on both military and moral grounds. He saw the French war as predominantly a military action to solve a political situation. He believed that Dulles and Radford were committing the cardinal sin of underestimating the enemy. He felt certain that the war could not be won on the cheap, by naval and air power alone, and that intervention would lead inevitably to a demand for his depleted ground troops, to be used in a jungle war under conditions far worse than those in Korea.

Without waiting to see whether his opposition would deter the advocates of intervention, Ridgway sent an army team of experts—engineers, medical officers, signal and communication specialists, officers experienced in combat—to Indochina to study and report on what logistic requirements a large-scale military operation there would entail. It showed that intervention would eventually demand more ground troops than had fought in Korea. A war would have to be fought from bases one to six thousand miles away, with great complexes constructed in the country at enormous cost: roads, harbors, docks, communication facilities, staging areas, warehouses. Neither France nor the natives could be counted on for real support. Jungle warfare would nullify the U.S. advantage in mechanized, mobile equipment. Draft calls would quadruple, to a hundred thousand a month. Defense costs would go up to perhaps $40 billion a year.

"I gave the report to Secretary Stevens," Ridgway says.

He passed it up through channels to President Eisenhower. There was no response from him. On May 17, 1954—eight days after the fall of Dien Bien Phu—I went to Acting Secretary of Defense Anderson. Secretary Stevens was present. I told them that my conscience obliged me to express an opinion no one had asked for, on what the consequences would be if we intervened in Indochina. I said that I had asked Lieutenant General Gavin, my operations and training officer, to prepare a short, factual logistic briefing on Indochina. I said that I had told General Wilton Persons and another officer on Eisenhower's staff that it was available if the President wished to see it.

Bob Anderson directed me to prepare a brief summary of my views, addressed to the Secretary of Defense, and Bob Stevens would sign it. This was done. A few days later I was requested to have someone give the logistic briefing to the President and a few of his aides. I gave it myself. The President said very little, asked several questions. It was apparent to me that, with his military experience, he understood the full implications of the briefing.

It was one episode in Ridgway's term as army chief that had a successful and happy ending. The President sided with Ridgway, and though he directed him to send a relatively small number of men to train the South Vietnamese, he overruled the proposal to use U.S. combat troops. General Collins wrote that intervention "was scotched on the recommendation of Matthew B. Ridgway," and he added that while he had no part in the decision, he agreed with it completely.

Ridgway retired, as he had intended to do, on June 30, 1955. He was not asked to serve a second term, and he was not offered, as was customary, another post. He was succeeded by his old friend and colleague Maxwell Taylor, who was cross-examined at length by Secretary Wilson on his readiness to carry out civilian orders even when they were contrary to his own views. Ridgway wrote a twelve-page farewell message to Secretary Wilson in which, in moderate language, he criticized the new defense policy and set forth his own beliefs and recommendations in a perilous world. Wilson classified his letter as confidential, but a young officer, without Ridgway's knowledge, gave it to the *New York Times,* where it appeared on July 14 and caused something of a sensation. When questioned by reporters, Wilson said that the document was "not very important."

Ridgway received a heavy volume of letters following his retirement and the publication of his message to Wilson. One letter, addressed to "Dear Matt," was early-vintage Dean Rusk, who in 1950–51 had been Assistant Secretary of State for Far Eastern Affairs. He wrote: "The historian will one day record how your personal leadership built a great army in Korea and saved your country from the humiliation of defeat through loss of morale in high places. Those few of us who know the full story will be forever grateful." Walter Lippman wrote: "You are among the few of whom one can say that they were among the first in war and among also the first in peace." The Washington *Post* said it felt "a twinge of sadness" at the retirement:

Throughout his career he had shown a rugged integrity. . . . [He] also may have supplied the questioning, the skepticism about the easy theories of immaculate war that forestalled rash American action at Dien Bien Phu. . . . Perhaps because he knows what the army would face, he also has spoken for world peace in insisting that new commitments be weighed against the cost. . . . Americans owe him a continued debt of gratitude.

He took the position of chairman and chief executive officer of the Mellon Institute of Industrial Research in Pittsburgh. In 1956, in collaboration with the writer-editor Harold H. Martin, he produced *Soldier,* one of the best and most readable of the many volumes of memoirs by

Allied generals. He retired again in 1960, at age sixty-five. He watched with dismay as President Kennedy, young and with new advisers, drifted aimlessly into deeper and deeper involvement in Vietnam, and then as President Johnson compounded that blunder. Robert Asprey, author of *War in the Shadows: The History of Guerilla Warfare*, wonders whether the Joint Chiefs and the President's advisers were ignorant of the 1954 Ridgway Report or simply ignored it. Whichever the case, he says, Ridgway's stubborn voice of caution and dissent was missing, and they did not use a study that might have saved them from what John Kenneth Galbraith has called "a massive miscalculation, perhaps the worst miscalculation in our history."

Ridgway wrote a second book, *The Korean War*, in 1967, a soldier's account of that action, and closed it with a sober expression of doubt that the country's political objectives in Southeast Asia harmonized with its real national interests. In articles in *Look* magazine (1966) and *Foreign Affairs* (1971) he called for a phased withdrawal from Vietnam. He did the same as one of a group of "Wise Men" at a "Crisis of Conscience" conference in March, 1968, called —and so named—by President Johnson.

After his second retirement, in 1960, Ridgway was able to devote more time to his family, and especially to his son Matty—he who had been born in Panama, learned to walk in Japan, and learned to talk in France. The family spent weeks together camping in the national forests, and under his father's fond tutelage Matty became a skilled woodsman. He was a handsome young man and did well in school, both as an athlete and in his studies.

Matty was graduated from Bucknell in June, 1971, and received his commission as a second lieutenant in the Army Reserve the same month. Then he left for a canoe camp at Lake Timagami in Ontario, where he was to act as a guide and counselor for teen-age boys on an eight-week canoe trip. During an early portage they were walking along a railroad track, Matt in the lead, a canoe over his head in Indian fashion, when a train came speeding down the track. The boys scrambled up an embankment to safety, but the train struck an end of Matty's canoe, knocked it around, and broke his neck.

The stunned parents flew to Canada. After a time they boarded a private plane that took them over the Lake of the Woods. With them they had Chaplain Gordon Mercer of the Canadian Armed Forces. As they neared the northern end of the lake the flare chute was opened, and, kneeling on the lurching floor of the plane, they shared a two-minute prayer. Then they committed the ashes of their son to the beautiful Canadian lake and forest country he had loved so dearly.

There is no consolation for such a tragedy, but General Ridgway and his wife have endured their sorrow with not unexpected courage. They take at least one long trip each year: in 1972 a photographic safari among the big-game herds in Kenya, Tanganyika, and Uganda; in 1973 a summer exploration cruise to the edge of the ice pack a thousand miles above Spitsbergen; in 1974 a return to Holland as guests of the Netherlands government at the thirtieth anniversary of the Eindhoven-Arnhem airdrop.

The general has a large library and reads a great deal —usually for an hour each day before an early breakfast —mostly history, some biography, no fiction, often a book in Spanish, his second language. One volume on his shelves is that definitive work on the evolution of the Vietnam disaster, *The Best and the Brightest* (1974) by David Halberstam. On the flyleaf the author, whom Ridgway has never met, has written: "For General Matthew Ridgway, the one hero of this book...." ☆

The Slaughter of the Buffalo
CONTINUED FROM PAGE 41

suits of clothes to the interview. As he later reported, Mooar's specific question to Dodge was "Major, if we cross into Texas, what will be the government's attitude towards us?" Even to cross Indian land was illegal by the terms of the Medicine Lodge Treaty, but it was the only way to get from Kansas to Texas, and besides it could be argued, technically, that a crossing would not be illegal if it were made over the so-called no man's land to the west of the actual Cheyenne-Arapaho reservation. On the other hand, they would have no license to hunt there, and Texans might feel differently about shooting their buffalo—not because the Texans were against killing buffalo, but because the presence of buffalo in the panhandle helped keep the Kiowas and Comanches out of central Texas settlements.

Mooar and Frazier soon found their caution unnecessary, however. Major Dodge, himself a sportsman and hunter, received them warmly and finally confided: "Boys, if I were a buffalo hunter, I would hunt where the buffaloes are." And thus was formalized the unwritten alliance between the hidemen and the United States Army.

The buffalo runners therefore agreed to carry out the next season's hunt high on the "Staked Plains" (El Llano Estacado) of the Texas panhandle, the vast, grassy plateau that rises abruptly from the flat lowlands. This would put them west of the Indian Territory and outside the Indians' hunting reserves, the northern part of which of course they had already depleted. Theoretically, the Indians should have no quarrel with them, except for the brief but necessary trespass, if indeed it were a trespass. The hunters knew, however, the Indians would not see it that way. As far as the Indians were concerned, all the buffalo south of the Arkansas River were theirs, and the whites had stolen from them. The heat for revenge was high; the presence of white hunters among the last herds of buffalo on the South

Plains would likely touch off a savage Indian war, and the hunters knew it.

Most of the hidemen spent the winter of 1873–74 holed up in Dodge City, but some of the hardier outfits wasted no time and headed for the Texas ranges that very fall. The Mooars, for example, reloaded their own wagons and hurried back, the dangers posed by the Indians notwithstanding. Also going south with his outfit was Billy Dixon, at twenty-three one of the ablest and most respected marksmen on the plains. The actual process of hunting the buffalo on the range that autumn was best explained by Wright Mooar himself, as quoted many years later in a book about the period:

> Each outfit would take a wagon, a keg of water, a roll of bedding, and a little grub and, with a four-mule team, would drive out on the divide between the North Palo Duro and the Canadian. There we would intercept the herds that were crossing, east to west, from the headwaters of Wolf Creek to the Blue and the Coldwater. We stayed there on the divide until we loaded out the wagon with hides and meat. We could haul 10,000 pounds when the ground was frozen. We would load, come back to camp, unload, and go back out again. We could keep track of the Wheelers' outfit [another team of hunters], and his of ours, by the sound of the guns. If either of us got into trouble, the sound of the buffalo guns would be interrupted with the reports of lighter guns.

The favorite gun of all the buffalo hunters was the Sharp's "Big Fifty" buffalo rifle, a .50-caliber octagonal-barrelled cannon that, with its 2,000 foot-pounds of muzzle energy, could send a heavy ball an astonishing distance. One model weighed sixteen pounds, but Mooar and most of the others preferred the lighter kinds. "I killed 6,500 buffaloes with my fourteen-pound gun," recalled Mooar, "and 14,000 with the eleven-pounder." Mooar and the other professionals always insisted on making their own bullets, melting their own lead and overloading the three-inch bottlenecked cartridges with up to 110 grains of powder. Ninety grains was standard, but the massive eight-sided barrels had no trouble handling the extra charge. A weapon of this type could kill the strongest buffalo at six hundred yards; some of them were equipped with 10x and 20x telescopes, and a well-placed ball could drop an animal at three quarters of a mile. Each man followed his own eccentricities in loading his gun, and it was possible to recognize almost any hunter on the plains merely by the peculiar "boom" of his Sharp's Fifty. One other rather grim article that each hunter carried with him at all times was his "bite," a Big Fifty cartridge emptied of its powder and filled with cyanide, guaranteeing a quick death infinitely preferable to the tortures devised by the Indians, and insurance as well against mutilation. Warriors would only scalp or "count coup" on a victim they had actually killed; the bodies of hunters who "bit the bite" were always found intact.

There were several techniques for slaughtering the buffalo, but the most effective, and therefore most favored, was the "stand." When a herd was found, the hunter would pick out an exposed place some hundreds of yards away from which he could fire in relative comfort and not alarm the animals. Setting up the forked rest sticks on which he set the heavy barrel of his buffalo gun, he first picked out and shot the leader of the herd. With no leader to start a stampede the animals milled about until the hunter shot as many as his skinners could handle. That done, the skinners would go out (the hunter usually had three or four in his employ) to rip off the hides. A good hunter could kill fifty animals in a stand before the herd bolted or wandered out of range. Billy Dixon, one of the best, "once took 120 hides without moving his rest sticks." Hunters making a stand generally killed only as many as their skinners could handle in a day. Frank H. Mayer, one of the last surviving buffalo runners, recalled not long before his death: "Killing more than we could use would waste buff, which wasn't important; it would also waste ammunition, which was."

If the government had lived up to its treaty obligations to protect the Indians from the buffalo hunters, there would have been little possibility of renewed warfare with the South Plains tribes. But such protection was not the government's policy, and it is difficult to imagine the privation the eradication of the buffalo caused among the Indians. In the first place, the primary year-round staple of the tribes' diet was dried buffalo meat, gathered when the hunting was good, then stored in sacks of dried buffalo skin. From the hides of the big, shaggy animals the Indians fashioned their clothing and the tepees they lived in, their war shields, cradles for their infants, even rude boats of hides stretched over willow saplings. They wove rope from the hair and stretched the tendons into bowstrings and thread. They fashioned the large bones into tools, rendered glue from the hoofs, even removed and dried the bladders to use as canteens. Brains were pounded into a pulp used as a tanning paste, as were extracts from fat and other organs. The horns were crafted into eating utensils; even the tails were dried to serve as war clubs and knife scabbards. And in addition to these practical uses the buffalo was the heart of the Indians' culture and religion. The South Plains Indians believed very simply that when all the buffalo were gone, their world would come to its end.

Most of the Indian agents, whose job it was to carry out government policy toward the Indians, were dismayed at the blatantly illegal destruction of the buffalo, but without army help the agents lacked the police power to bring the poachers to justice. Only once, apparently, did an agent manage to act against the hidemen. In early February, 1874, the Cheyenne-Arapaho agent, John D. Miles, caused the arrest of some eleven buffalo hunters who were trespassing on Indian land, but the hunters evidently did some

Skinners who travelled with each hunter took nothing from the carcasses but the hides and the tongues. The tongues (though soldiers fed them to dogs) were salable and were dried on racks.

persuasive talking, for Miles soon let them go again and even returned their outfits to them. "They are all very poor," wrote Miles, "and they say that the cries of their children *for bread* is what induced them to engage in the chase . . . I have no disposition to disbelieve. . . ." He added, rather naively, that he believed the hunters had learned their lesson and that the incident would deter other hidemen from entering the reservation.

Secretary of the Interior Columbus Delano stated the government's view in his annual reports of 1872 and 1873:

> In our intercourse with the Indians it must always be borne in mind that we are the most powerful party. . . . We are assuming, and I think with propriety, that our civilization ought to take the place of their barbarous habits. We therefore claim the right to control the soil they occupy, and we assume it is our duty to coerce them, if necessary, into the adoption and practice of our habits and customs. . . . I would not seriously regret the total disappearance of the buffalo from our western prairies, in its effect upon the Indians, regarding it rather as a means of hastening their sense of dependence upon the products of the soil.

Yet the majority of the Indians were in fact willing to give the white man's road a chance. The Arapahos, for instance, had been docile since the Medicine Lodge Treaty. Among the Cheyennes there had not been an all-out war for six years—since 1868—and in 1869 that tribe's most influential spokesman for peace, Chief Little Robe, had actually banished from his camps the militant Dog Soldier Society. Its members drifted northward for a while, and when they returned, the peace chiefs—Little Robe, White Shield, Stone Calf, and Old Whirlwind—were successful in controlling them. The Kiowas and Comanches had been officially tractable for an even longer period. When the Medicine Lodge council convened in October of 1867, its commissioners agreed that "the testimony satisfies us that since October, 1865 [when they had signed an earlier treaty], the Kiowas, Comanches, and Apaches have substantially complied with their treaty stipulation entered into at that time at the mouth of the Little Arkansas."

Though the wilder war chiefs continued to sporadically make forays into Texas, most of the Kiowas and Comanches admitted that war against the whites was a hopeless proposition, especially after 1872, the year some of the chiefs went to Washington and saw the power of the whites for themselves. Among the Kiowas tempers flared when those chiefs who stayed home refused to believe the tales of huge cities and giant stone tepees so large that all the Kiowa tribe could sit in a single one. When Thomas Battey, the Quaker schoolteacher to the Kiowas, produced stereo views of the sights in the East, the war chiefs who had been skeptical before were struck dumb with amazement. As Battey reported the scene, Chief Sun Boy, who had been to Washington, said angrily to his fellow tribesmen: "What you think now? You think all lie now? You think all chiefs who been to Washington fools now?" The warriors put their fingers over their open mouths. "Look! see what a mighty powerful people they are! We fools! We don't know anything! We just like wolves running wild on the plains!"

By 1874 most of the South Plains Indians were ready to come in to the agencies and learn the white man's ways, but their own primitiveness worked against them. The Kiowas, for instance, would not permit a census of their people because of a tribal superstition that made them deathly afraid of being counted.

But tribal superstitions were minor indeed compared to the basic problem. Without their buffalo the Indians were entirely dependent on government rations for their survival, and when these rations were not forthcoming, the Indians sat at the agencies and quite literally starved. Had the government only provided them with some alternative source of food and supply, their transition to the white man's ways, though painful and clumsy, might well have been bloodless. But to obtain food for them the federal authorities relied on private contractors, a system that never worked well even in the best of times. In the case of the South Plains tribes it all but broke down completely, and during the blizzard-stricken winter of 1873–74 the Indians were forced to slaughter large numbers of their ponies just to stay alive. Given insufficient provisions at the agencies when they stayed there, and accused of raiding when they left to hunt buffalo, the Indians' attempt to follow the white road was virtually hopeless.

Even Nelson A. Miles, who during the war prosecuted his campaign against the Cheyennes with all the fervor of an ambitious colonel after his star, wrote many years later:

> One of the strongest causes of unrest among [the Indians] . . . was the fact that the promises made to induce them to go on to reservations were not always carried out by the government authorities. They had been removed from . . . the ranges of the buffalo, but under distinct treaty stipulation that they were to be provided with shelter, clothing, and sustenance. . . . They were sometimes for weeks without their rations. Their annual allowance of food was usually exhausted in six or seven months. . . .

By early 1874 the food-supply problem was becoming more and more critical. In March the chief clerk of the Central Superintendency toured the agencies and reported "very discouragingly" on the supply situations, especially at Fort Sill, the Kiowa-Comanche agency. He wrote that even Satanta and Lone Wolf, conceded to be the Kiowas' two biggest "problem" chiefs where pacification was concerned, ". . . are peaceably disposed, but the want of something to eat at the very commencement of the [spring] raiding season seems to me most suicidal."

During April and May, Agent James M. Haworth also wrote urgent letters about the lack of supplies. "Our sustenance is getting very low," he warned the Commissioner of Indian Affairs on April 8, "& unless more is purchased soon we will be left with nothing to give them and they caused to seek it in other channels, which would be very unfortunate at this season of the year." On April 20 Haworth reported to Enoch Hoag at the Central Superintendency: "This week's issue will exhaust our supply of flour, which now amounts to only half rations. My teams are gone on the hunt for sugar, and coffee. I hope to have them back by issue day. . . ." His May 6 report said almost wistfully: "Issue day is almost here, only one night off, and the sugar and coffee not here. . . ."

Such was the situation when Big Bow, a Kiowa war chief, came in for rations on May 7. Obviously discouraged, the chief said, according to Haworth,

> We come in from our camps on issue day, to get our rations, only we find little here. We carry that home, divide around among the people. It is soon gone, and our women and children begin to cry with hunger, and that makes our hearts feel bad. A white man's heart would soon get bad to see his wife and children crying for something to eat, when he had nothing to give them.

A couple of weeks later Haworth indicated the lack of food was also responsible for the disaffection of the Comanches, stating that it was becoming increasingly difficult for those peaceably inclined to maintain any influence when keeping the "good path" was rewarded with hunger and privation. "If I had supplies on hand," he wrote, "to help those who wanted to do right, it would be a great help to them. . . . Our scarcity of supplies is one of our greatest—in fact, is *the* greatest drawback, in governing these people. Give me plenty of supplies, and I will exert a controlling influence over them."

At the Darlington agency, meanwhile, Agent John Miles was experiencing every bit as difficult a time obtaining food for his Cheyennes and Arapahos. On March 21, 1874, an opportunity presented itself for Miles to pacify a large portion of the Cheyennes, as 140 lodges came into the agency, led by Chiefs Minimic, White Shield, and Old Whirlwind. With them, very significantly, was White Horse, head chief of the historically implacable Dog Soldiers. It was, wrote Miles, the very first time any of the Dog Soldiers had come in for rations; they said the buffalo were scarce, and Miles believed they would stay in as long as he could feed them. But, he wrote ominously to Hoag in begging for more supplies, "We will soon be out of rations, and thou can then judge of our situation." Ten days later the warning took on an increased urgency: "We now have at this Agency over 500 lodges of Cheyennes and Arapahoes. . . ." Only Grey Beard and his sixty lodges were still out, and they were expected any day. "Our coffee, sugar, & bacon is exhausted," Miles continued, "and the beef contractor is *considering whether* he can furnish any more beef. . . . We cannot afford to let these people leave the Agency just at this time. They could not find buffalo nearer than 150 miles, and that in the direction of western Texas, just the place that we do not want them to go. . . ."

Miles was, in addition, expecting a visit from a party of thirty Northern Arapahos under Chief Plenty Wolf. "They must be treated well," he wrote, or they could persuade his own Indians to forsake the agency and return to the plains, a danger heightened by Plenty Wolf's report on the disappearance of the buffalo. His band's trek southward had taken some three months, during which time "they saw but two buffalo en route."

No additional rations came, however. By April 4 Grey Beard had arrived, accompanied by another of the less friendly chiefs, Heap of Birds, which meant that virtually every Southern Cheyenne and Arapaho belonging to Miles's agency was present, accounted for, and hungry: "It is *very important* NOW that these people be *fed*!"

His ration supply dwindled away steadily, until by the second week in May, Miles had, however reluctantly, been obliged to release those who wished to go west and find what buffalo they could. Thus, to Miles's intense frustration and dismay, the Cheyennes were forced to compete with the white buffalo-hunters from Kansas for the last large segment of the Great Southern herd of buffalo, whose migration was at that time carrying it across the Staked Plains of the Texas panhandle.

Hunger, then, was the principal force that drove the South Plains Indians back on the warpath in the spring of 1874. It was not, however, their only cause for anger.

Probably the second greatest cause, and one of the least studied, was the havoc wrought among the Indian pony herds by white horse-thieves from Kansas and Texas. The Treaty of Medicine Lodge specifically provided: "If bad men among the whites . . . shall commit any wrong upon the person or property of the Indians, the United States will, upon proof made to the agent and forwarded to the Commissioner of Indian Affairs at Washington City, proceed at once to cause the offender to be arrested and punished according to the laws of the United States, and also re-imburse the injured person for the loss sustained." Where enforcement was concerned, "United States" meant the United States Army, yet it was in the face of a studied lack of cooperation that Agents Miles and Haworth labored to exhaustion to stamp out the theft of Indian stock.

The Commissioner of Indian Affairs, Edward P. Smith, did make an attempt to get law-enforcement officers into the Indian Territory, but bogged down in a tangle of jurisdictional red tape. Only two deputy marshals were authorized to patrol literally thousands of square miles of wild country; the raids on Indian stock by white outlaws continued unabated. The effect of this stealing on the Indians is shown graphically in the theft on about March 11, 1874, of forty-three ponies from the herd of Little Robe, one of the most consistently peaceful Cheyenne chiefs. It is widely accepted that this incident was important in putting many of the Cheyennes on the warpath, and as Agent Miles observed: "The Chiefs are very much provoked and discouraged . . . and express the fear that, should nothing be done . . . and another raid be made upon them, that it will be impossible for them to restrain their young men from making a like raid on the frontier of Kansas."

That was an understatement; the Cheyennes were furious, and an examination of agency correspondence shows that white inaction was actually more crass than has ever been admitted, for in this case the Indians knew the precise identity of the thieves. The agent, of course, did what he could. In response to Miles's stern "This matter must have attention," Superintendent Hoag sent a transcript of the marshals' report to Kansas Governor Osborn, who promised that the guilty men would be punished—if they should happen to be found.

White horse-thieves were also a chronic problem at the Kiowa-Comanche agency. Texans constantly stole horses from those of the Kiowas and Comanches registered at Fort Sill who were peaceable. At one point Haworth was moved to write:

> Since the Indians have camped near the Agency over one hundred head of their stock has been stolen and taken into Texas—and none recovered . . . I have made an arrangement with the sheriff of Clay County, into which [the thieves] often go, to apprehend and bring them back here, for which I am to pay him a fair compensation, not exceeding ten dollars a head for returned horses.

Whether payment of such bounty with bureau funds was fully legitimate is not clear, but it does show to what lengths Haworth was willing to go to keep white outlaws from robbing his Indian charges.

In addition to their actual raids on Indian pony herds, the white thieves were also aggravating the general tension by trying to lay the blame for their own crimes on Indians. For instance, when they murdered another white, they often scalped their victim in Indian fashion. That they managed to stir up the already inflamed tempers of the frontier population against the Indians is shown by a report dated June 19, 1874, from Major C. E. Compton, then commanding Fort Dodge, Kansas, to the effect that the countryside was even then seized with a panic from just such a murder. "That Indians committed this crime," the major wrote, "I do not believe but am strongly impressed with the belief that horse thieves—who of late have become such a pest to this neighborhood—are responsible for the deed, the scalping having been done with a view of shielding themselves."

Many of the whites who stole the Indians' horses were also guilty of smuggling them liquor and illegally selling them guns, a highly lucrative trade for the whites, by which they netted a small fortune in buffalo robes.

Altogether, it became only a matter of time before some incident occurred that would touch off a major war. In December a raiding party of Comanches and Kiowas, understandably sick of living off an inadequate agency dole, sortied for Mexico. They had returned as far as the Double Mountain Fork of the Brazos River when they were intercepted and attacked by Lieutenant Charles Hudson with a sizable force of soldiers. Eleven of the Indians were killed and, in the rout, abandoned, but three of the casualties were especially incendiary: one was the uncle of a young medicine man named Isa-tai, of the Quahadi Comanches. The other two were Tauankia, the favorite son of Lone Wolf, principal chief of the Kiowas, and his cousin Guitain, the son of Lone Wolf's brother, also a chief, Red Otter.

When Lone Wolf heard of the disaster, he went wild with grief. He hacked off his hair, maimed his body fearfully, slaughtered his horses, burned his possessions, and vowed to get even. Red Otter and Lone Wolf's wife visited Haworth, explaining that Lone Wolf would calm down once the shock had passed; but when the old chief went to Texas to bury his son and was himself attacked by soldiers and forced to abandon the body once more, he was beyond the reach of reason. He would have war.

Chief Lone Wolf, like all the South Plains Indians, had

only the dimmest notion of the historical forces working upon his people, but by the spring of 1874 nearly all the camps were smoldering hotbeds of resentment. As they understood it, the Medicine Lodge Treaty of 1867 had guaranteed their reservations to them, for their free, unhampered, and "exclusive" use, but the white buffalo-poachers had destroyed practically every buffalo herd in the northern part of the territory. It was Indian land and Indian buffalo, and the whites had stolen from them. The government had promised to provide for them and had lied. Except for their agents, who they discovered had no real power, Washington did nothing. It was now evident to the Indians that the white government had no intention of carrying out its part of the Medicine Lodge bargain.

By the spring of 1874 the situation was ready to explode. In the tepees there was talk of war and killing, of driving the white man from the land, but as yet there had been little action. The Indians had surrounded and picked off isolated parties of buffalo poachers for years, but there had never been any general offensive, partly because they did not have any leader capable of organizing such an offensive. During the spring of 1874, however, such a leader finally emerged, in the person of Isa-tai, the adolescent but highly volatile medicine man of the wild Quahadi band of the Comanches.

He was a young warrior, deep in grief for his uncle, who was one of those killed in the Hudson skirmish in Texas. As yet he was untried in battle, but throughout the year 1873 one thing had become certain to the Comanches: his medicine was strong. He said he had brought the dead back to life and that he was immune to the bullets of the white man. That in itself was not particularly impressive, since other great shamans had claimed those feats, but here Isa-tai surpassed the others. He claimed, and was supported by witnesses, that he could swallow and vomit forth at will wagonloads of cartridges. He said he had ascended above the clouds, where he had communed with the Great Spirit. This also witnesses swore to. Many believed in him. A few may have doubted his self-proclaimed messianic role in driving away the white men, preferring to see him as just another young buck trying to get up a revenge raid for a slain relative—as indeed it was proper by the Indian code for him to do—but no one could doubt that early in 1873, before the uncle was killed, when a brilliant comet had appeared, it was Isa-tai who predicted it would disappear in five days' time. The comet vanished on schedule. Later on it was Isa-tai who had predicted the blizzards of the 1873–74 winter, and that had firmly established his reputation. The medicine of Isa-tai was strong indeed, and the young man was doing his best to incite a war against the whites.

By May his influence had grown to the degree that he did an unprecedented thing: he sent out runners, summoning all the bands of the Comanches to attend a Sun Dance. It was a bold step, for the Comanches had never even been assembled all in one place before, let alone made tribal medicine. The Sun Dance was a ritual foreign to their culture, although among the other South Plains tribes it was an annual occurrence. In Isa-tai's mind the move was probably to accomplish two things: first, to capitalize on his newfound notoriety by assembling an audience to whom to preach his antiwhite doctrine and, second, to recruit the war party.

News of the young firebrand Isa-tai reached Agent Haworth, who wrote of him, tongue in cheek, to Hoag: "They have a new Medicine Man, who can accomplish wonders. Horse Back says he can furnish them an inexhaustible supply of cartridges, suited for any gun, from his stomach. Certainly a very valuable man to have around in time of war. He can also raise the dead, having recently done so." In a much more serious vein he also sent a peace feeler to the Quahadi camp, but their answer was not encouraging, telling him, in effect, that if he kept out of the way he would not be hurt. If he interfered, he and everyone else the Quahadis could find at the agency would be put to death.

Precisely what happened at the war council has never been learned with great certainty. Most definite information about it came from the Penatekas and the friendly Yapparika chiefs, Quirts Quip and Ho-weah, who bolted the ceremony and returned to the agency, although they did so at no small risk to themselves, as the hostile faction threatened to shoot their horses and strand them afoot if they did not commit themselves to the war movement. Haworth did learn that Isa-tai had staged a mystical display of his magic, utterly convincing the skeptics that they would receive divine protection in their war effort. He also learned from Quirts Quip that Mexican Comancheros were present at the encampment and that the liberal consumption of whiskey served mostly to harden the stand of the war faction, though they tended to make up their minds in drunken confusion. The leaders, said Quirts Quip, "have a great many hearts . . . Make up their minds at night for one thing and get up in the morning entirely changed." In addition, Ho-weah told Haworth that the Cheyennes had ridden into the council brandishing no fewer than eighty mint-new breechloading rifles.

During the ceremonies, which were held at the very fringe of the reservation, some of the war party slipped back in to Fort Sill and stole about fifty head of stock from the agency corral. Grim and sobered, Haworth reported the incident, adding: "I am at a loss to account for their actions, though [they were] much disappointed at the shortness of their rations." Still he hoped, as he had written before, that "this cloud will, like many others since I came here, pass away, without a storm."

This time, however, he was wrong. ☆

The Battle of Lake Erie CONTINUED FROM PAGE 20

less of my feelings." Perry had a quick temper, and he most likely regretted the letter after he sent it; in any event, the request—no doubt to Perry's great relief—was not taken seriously. The Secretary replied in a temperate letter, saying: "A change of commander, under existing circumstances, is equally inadmissible as it respects the interest of the service and your own reputation. It is right that you should reap the harvest which you have sown."

It was weeks before Perry could reap his harvest, but they were valuable weeks. He cruised around the lake, exercising his crews and getting the feel of his squadron. He met with General Harrison, who, on September 1, sent him a hundred Kentucky soldiers with their fabulous long rifles; the lanky, skeptical men poked around the ships and made a general nuisance of themselves. They brought Perry's complement up to four hundred and ninety. Still weak from his sickness yet anxious for action, Perry based his squadron in Put-in Bay, a fine harbor in the Bass Islands, some thirty miles southeast of Amherstburg.

Barclay knew Perry was nearby, but he was loath to fight him, for his own ships were desperately undermanned. He had a fine new brig, the *Detroit*, built at Amherstburg. Yeo was no more anxious to give over guns than he was men, and so the ship had been constructed without her builders having any idea of what sort of armament she was to carry. Eventually Barclay armed her with field guns borrowed from General Procter. There were six different types of cannon among her nineteen guns, which would mean inconceivable difficulties with ammunition supply once the fighting started. By now Procter was desperate; thousands of his Indian allies were consuming rations, and until the Americans were dislodged from the lake, no more food could come in. Barclay was faced with the choice of abandoning the fleet or going out to fight. For a British naval officer that was no choice at all. When Barclay reluctantly weighed anchor late in the day on September 9, there was one day's supply of flour left at Amherstburg.

On that night Perry called his officers aboard his ship and discussed the battle he knew was imminent. Barclay's strongest ships were the *Detroit* and the *Queen Charlotte*, which mounted seventeen guns. These would be engaged by the *Lawrence*, Perry's flagship, and her sister ship, the *Niagara*, which Perry had placed under the command of Jesse Elliott. Perry drew up a line of battle and

Captain Robert Heriot Barclay
Ohio History, JULY, 1963

then, paraphrasing Nelson's great dictum, said: "If you lay your enemy alongside, you cannot be out of place." The officers returned to their ships, and a full autumn moon came out and rolled across the sky. Living things chittered and peeped on the shore of the harbor, and the ships lay motionless on the water in the bright, still night.

The next morning at sunup the lookouts sighted the British fleet, and Perry stood out for open water. It was a fine, cloudless day, with fluky breezes that eventually steadied and swung around to the southeast, giving the American ships the weather gauge —the important ability to force or decline battle as they chose. The schooner *Chippewa* led the enemy line, followed by Barclay's flagship, the *Detroit*, the brig *Queen Charlotte*, the brig *Hunter* of ten guns, the schooner *Lady Prevost*, and the sloop *Little Belt*. Perry accordingly arranged his line so that the *Lawrence* was in the van, with the schooners *Ariel* and *Scorpion* standing by her weather bow, the *Caledonia* next, to fight the *Hunter*, and then the *Niagara*, with which Elliott was to engage the *Queen Charlotte*. The gunboat-schooners *Somers*, *Porcupine*, and *Tigress* and the sloop *Trippe* would take on the *Lady Prevost* and the *Little Belt*. Dobbins should have been there in the schooner *Ohio*, but he had been sent to Erie to pick up supplies.

The American ships cleared for action; stands of cutlasses were set up on deck, shot was placed near the guns, and the hatches were closed save for a ten-inch-square aperture through which the powder charges would be passed. Sand was sprinkled on the decks so that the sailors could keep their footing when the blood began to flow. Perry brought the ship's papers, wrapped in lead, to the ship's surgeon and told him to throw them overboard should the *Lawrence* be forced to strike. Sometime during the morning he hoisted his battle flag, a blue banner bearing the dying words attributed to Captain Lawrence: "Don't Give up the Ship." It was a curious slogan, in a way, filled as it was with negative implications—the ship, after all, had been given up—but the crew cheered when they saw it unfurl in the light breeze.

Then there was nothing more to be done. Perry turned to one of his officers. "This is the most important day of my life," he said.

The British fleet had been freshly painted, and the ships looked clean and formidable, bearing toward the Americans in the sunny morning. At about quarter to twelve the sailors on the *Lawrence* heard a band playing what sounded like "Rule Britannia," the music faint across the water. There was an enormous weight of reputation riding with those English men-of-war on a lake in the middle of North America. When the band was finished, the *Detroit* fired a ranging shot. A few minutes later she fired another, which hit the *Lawrence*. The two ships were still a mile apart, and Perry realized that Barclay had the edge on him. All but two of Perry's guns were 32-pounder carronades, short-barrelled pieces that were deadly at short range but not good for much beyond 250 yards. Barclay, on the other hand, was well supplied with long guns. Perry's only hope was to engage Barclay closely, so he held his fire while the two ships closed, and the Briton picked his ship apart in a ghastly sort of target practice.

After a half hour the *Lawrence*'s rigging was almost useless, but Perry was close enough for his guns to take effect. The *Lawrence* opened fire, but she was virtually unsupported; she had sailed into action accompanied only by two small schooners. Far away through the smoke could be seen the *Niagara*, an idle spectator to the savage fight that was taking shape. Jesse Duncan Elliott had not yet begun to fight. Nor did he intend to, it seemed to the sailors on the *Lawrence*. The *Queen Charlotte*, finding that the *Niagara* would not come within range, now ran down on the *Lawrence*, and Perry soon found himself being fired on by some forty guns.

The destruction on the decks of the *Lawrence* was appalling. The air was filled with iron and great jagged splinters of wood, and the wounded tottered below faster than Usher Parsons, the surgeon, could treat them. "It seemed," he said, "as though heaven and earth were at loggerheads." John Brooks, the affable and popular lieutenant of marines and the handsomest man in the fleet, had his hip carried away by a cannonball and lay on the deck in agony, begging for a pistol with which to kill himself. Lying next to him, Samuel Hambleton, the purser, who was also wounded, took a verbal disposition of his will before the lieutenant died. The wounded crawled away to hide, but there was no safe, stout corner in the hastily built brig. Parsons was helping a midshipman to his feet after dressing a wound in his arm when the boy was torn out of his hands by a shot that smashed through the hull. Five cannonballs passed through the cabin where he was working. Blood spilled on the deck faster than men could throw sand on it, and sailors slipped and fell as they strained at the guns. The hammocks were shot apart, and the scraps of cloth that filled them danced in the smoky air like snowflakes. They settled on the bloody head of Lieutenant John Yarnall, Perry's second-in-command, and gave him the appearance of a huge owl as he kept the guns manned and working. Spars and rigging tumbled down from aloft, round shot hulled the ship again and again, men fell dead and were clawed apart by canister; and through it all the ship's dog, a small black spaniel, wailed and keened.

Sir James Lucas Yeo
NATIONAL PORTRAIT GALLERY, LONDON

Courage takes strange forms. It is said that Perry suffered a psychopathic fear of cows and would splash across a muddy road to avoid going near one of the innocuous beasts; but here he was, in the center of and bearing full responsibility for what was undoubtedly the worst place on earth at the moment, and he was utterly composed. An hour and a half into the chaotic afternoon he appeared at the skylight over the sickbay and calmly asked Parsons to spare him one of his assistants. He returned six times and finally, with all the assistants gone, asked if there were any wounded who could pull a rope. A few men actually dragged themselves back to the deck. But it was no use.

By 2:30 P.M., after an almost unbelievable defense, there was not a gun working on the *Lawrence*, and 80 per cent of her crew were down. And off out of range the *Niagara* still stood undamaged; Parsons says that many of the wounded cursed her in their last words.

Nobody will ever know what was going through Jesse Duncan Elliott's mind as he watched his sister ship get hammered into a listing ruin. He was some years older than Perry and felt that he should have had command of the squadron, and his jealousy may have been such that, like John Paul Jones's mad ally Captain Landais, he stood back waiting for his superior to be killed so that he could come in at the end of the fight and claim the victory. Much later his apologists would give the insufficient explanation that he was simply obeying orders by keeping the line of battle intact. The *Caledonia* was a slow sailor, and he was stuck behind her, reluctant to leave his station. Whatever the reason, as the *Lawrence*'s last gun stopped firing Elliott did leave the line and pass to windward of the ruined flagship. He was sure that Perry was dead, and it is a pity that there is no clear record of his reactions when Perry clambered up over the side of the *Niagara* and stood facing him.

On board the *Lawrence* Perry, miraculously unhurt, had determined that there still was a ship's boat, also miraculously unhurt. He had hauled down the "Don't Give up the Ship" battle flag—but not the American flag—and took it with him as he climbed into the boat, leaving Yarnall in command of the ship and the nine men still fit for duty. Thickly banked powder smoke covered him for part of the way as he made for the *Niagara*, but for most of the fifteen-minute journey the water around him was roiled with musketry and round shot. But Perry made it through unhurt.

As he climbed aboard Elliott's ship he saw, with "unspeakable pain," Yarnall lower the flag of the *Lawrence* in surrender. But it did not stay lowered for long, and the British never had a chance to take possession of the ship. Perry exchanged a word or two with Elliott, sent him back in the *Law-*

89

rence's dinghy to bring up the gunboats, and then, taking command of the *Niagara,* steered her toward the *Detroit.*

The British had taken quite a mauling before they finally silenced the *Lawrence.* A Canadian prisoner who visited the *Detroit* a month after the battle wrote that "it would be impossible to place a hand upon that broadside which had been exposed to the enemy's fire without covering some portion of a wound, either from grape, round, canister, or chain shot." Barclay was down—his remaining arm had been disabled and he had other wounds as well—and many of his officers were dead. The *Detroit* had gotten tangled up with the *Queen Charlotte* and could not get clear. The British were expecting the American fleet to sail away, leaving them their hard-won prize of the derelict *Lawrence.* Most of them, then, must have known that the game was up when they saw the *Niagara* with all sail set and hardly a scratch on her bearing down upon them. The American ship passed between the *Detroit* and the *Hunter,* her guns double-shotted, both broadsides booming out. It was enough. The gunboats were coming up, the *Niagara* had every gun in action, and the day was lost. At about three o'clock Barclay struck his colors.

Perry—hatless, filthy, his breeches black with smoke and blood—thought of General Harrison waiting on his word. He found an old envelope and wrote on the back of it: "DEAR GENL: We have met the enemy, and they are ours—two ships, two brigs, one schooner, and one sloop. Yours with great respect and esteem, O. H. PERRY."

Perry returned to the *Lawrence* that afternoon to receive the surrender of the British officers. As he climbed aboard a very few unwounded men, the surgeon among them, came forward to greet him. He stared speechlessly at the survivors and the carnage around him. When the British came aboard, he quietly refused their swords and inquired after Captain Barclay. Forty-one British had been killed, and ninety-four wounded. The Americans had suffered twenty-seven killed and ninety-six wounded, most of them on the terribly ravaged *Lawrence.* Four men had died on Elliott's ship.

Soon after Harrison got word of Perry's triumph, he started out after Procter. Perry ferried his men across the now friendly lake. When Procter got news of the outcome of the battle, he realized that his situation was hopeless. He retreated, but not fast enough, and Harrison caught up with him and beat him decisively at the Battle of the Thames. Detroit and the Northwest were regained for good. As Washington Irving said in a biography of Perry that he whipped out a few weeks after the victory: "The last roar of cannon that died along the shores of Lake Erie was the expiring note of British domination."

There was no question of the decisive results of the battle, but controversy over Elliott's role in it arose almost immediately and did not subside for thirty years. Perry, perhaps simply relieved and ebullient over the victory, mentioned Elliott favorably in his official report to the Secretary of the Navy. There were mutterings from Perry's subordinates when the two captains each got an equal share out of the $225,000 prize money for the capture of Barclay's fleet, and later an enraged Perry retracted his initial statement when it became evident that Elliott felt he had not received enough credit.

Barclay returned to London and faced a court-martial, which acquitted him with honor, although his only subsequent command was a brief one on a tiny bomb vessel. A London magazine, reporting the incident, indicated that shortly before Perry left the *Lawrence,* Elliott was making away from the battle. When this report reached the States, it meant a court of inquiry for Elliott—a hasty affair in which nothing was really decided.

Bell captured from the Queen Charlotte
PERRY MEMORIAL HOUSE, ERIE, PA.

Storm clouds always gathered thickest around Elliott's head. In 1818 he challenged Perry to a duel. Perry in turn filed charges against Elliott and demanded his court-martial, but President Monroe pigeonholed the matter; and the next year Perry died, killed by a fever he had contracted while on duty along the South American coast. Elliott continued to court controversy, and in 1839 the whole thing blew up again when James Fenimore Cooper published a history of the Navy in which he sought to justify Elliott's behavior. It never was conclusively settled, though Elliott struck off a medal for Cooper. The rest of his career was an amalgam of duels and challenges and courts-martial. He flickered in and out of favor with successive administrations and was in command of the Philadelphia Navy Yard when he died in 1845.

But despite all the creaky rationale formulated by Elliott's friends, the day was Perry's and Perry's alone. Through his own desperate initiative he had, at the very last moment, come through the smoke to win a lost battle. Henry Adams summed it up at the end of his description of the action: "No process of argument... could deprive Perry of the fame justly given him by the public, or detract from the splendor of his reputation as the hero of the war. More than any other battle of the time, the victory on Lake Erie was won by the courage and obstinacy of a single man."

As for Daniel Dobbins, he spent the rest of his life on the Lakes, navigating them for forty years and never, he liked to boast, losing so much as a spar. When the President awarded a sword to each midshipman and sailing master who served well on Lake Erie, Dobbins wrote saying that he would like one too. But he was told that since he had not been in the battle, he was not eligible, and he never got his sword. ☆

Ed: A Black Sharecropper's Story

CONTINUED FROM PAGE 13

window, I saw more men. I hadn't done anythin. And my little girl was too small.

I seen a Chevrolet settin out on the road.

Just walkin, walkin every which a way in my house, I didn't know what in the world to do.

"Lord have mercy," my wife cry. "Turn to the Lord."

They sure scared a fit on me. I wasn't thinkin about prayin.

They kept a callin, "Ed, come on out."

"I ain't comin out there. Who is it?"

"Josh Lawson."

I thought I heard "The Law." I ask him, "Who did you say that is?" My sisters both stand straight up in their double bed.

"Josh Lawson." He a bailiff. I knowed him.

"Light you a lamp."

"No, I don't need no light."

"Come on out here."

"No."

"Put your shoes on."

"All right." I set there and put my shoes on. That give me a little time to study. I had a .38 pistol and a good shotgun, but I didn't have nare cartridge and nare shell.

"Open the door."

I was shakin so bad. I crack open the door. There was a man standin with his back to the wall right next to the door. I look out right into his face. I shot the door back.

Now Josh Lawson seed I wasn't comin out unless he drug me out. "I'm lookin for McLeod," he say. "You seen McLeod?"

"Yeah, I seed him. He come by here this evenin with my brother."

"I'm comin in to search for him."

I open the door, and he come on in. I had one closet. He jump backwards up in that closet. He make a show of lookin around.

"Ed, you got any good drinkin liquor?"

"No, I don't drink liquor."

They run for the car because they knowed there was too many of them for the inside of Mr. Lawson's Chevrolet. Some could hang on to the runnin boards, and the last one or two would have to stick on the hood. Off they went to search the other colored people's houses.

After they left, I went to my brother's house. I want him and the other colored families to know the bailiff was comin.

They had done got at Homer before they come to my house. "I was so scared I butted my head against the wall tryin to kill myself," he say.

And they had been to my brother-in-law Tommy's house. He swore he wasn't scared. "Shoot, no!" But I know he was.

McLeod's mother-in-law had a bunch of cows in the barn, and he just went in there and lay down amongst them. He sneaked off, and I haven't seen him since.

Me and none of my people did anythin the next day. We just laid around.

—◆◆◆—

I had got to missin my Model T, so in 1932 I followed the style and made me a Hoover buggy. To do that you took the front axle of a Model T Ford and the two front wheels, and a lot of folks use the front seat with springs out of the car. It was drawn by a horse or mule and rode good with rubber tires.

Ours come in handy that summer, when Highway 280 was paved. We would go to town and buy groceries and my wife cooked them and I went up and down the highway in our buggy askin the workers which want to order a plate for noontime. We didn't earn much money, but we sure ate good.

Later I got to work on 280 with the PWA. If you had even a bank of taters and they knowed it or if a boss man said he could take care of you, you couldn't get on.

I've seen a lot of work on Highway 280. When I was a boy, one of the houses we lived in was high on a hill near an old wagon road. Me and my sister Rose would set in the yard and watch the convicts gradin it with picks and shovels and mattockses and grubbin hoes. They wasn't suppose to talk with nobody, but they was good at sidlin alongside someone. "Don't never come to the chain gang, boy." I didn't want to go there. When the men was whipped down in the swamp, we could hear them hollerin clean back to our house.

To grade the road men took the hills down by shovels. Standin in two lines, the convicts would face each other, every man with a shovel. A mule and wagon would be driv between them lines. When the wagons got to the bottom, they would be loaded.

Say there was a hole the chain-gang captain want to fill up. He'd put his foot in the hole. "Put that dirt on my foot." The men wouldn't pick up a shovelful like they did when they was throwin dirt on the wagon, just a thin layer. They could throw that much a pretty good ways.

Shovelin and throwin and singin:

Cap'n, Cap'n, has the money come?
None of your business, I don't owe you none.

They'd soon get the hole filled.

Then most of the colored couldn't look at a sheet of music and sing by notes. But the colored man had his own music in his mouth. If you can get up the spirit in a big

91

group, it will make you feel good. The burden will lift.

In July, 1932, I got me one of the first eight-hour jobs that ever come to Abbeville in Mr. Julian Graham's sawmill. They was payin five dollars a day wages. Mr. Graham got to be the mayor of Abbeville.

The biggest thing about that sawmill was the whistle. People on the farm had always worked from sunup to dark. At the mill they'd blow the whistle for lunch and for knockin off in the evenin. The people livin in town heard the whistle all the time. It got so when they went out to do farm jobs, they just didn't want to work after that whistle blow.

At first everybody who could got them a job at that mill. There was the whistle. And there was another reason. Mr. Graham didn't want his hands locked up where they couldn't work. Anybody else's hands he was glad to be hard on when they come to town and done somethin called wrong. But he want his'n to get off light.

The trouble was the work at the mill was so hard you couldn't hardly make an eight-hour day. I pulled a cross saw there before the pugwood saw run by a little motor come out. Pullin that saw all day long, you had to be a man young and strong to stand it. The mosquitoes and red bugs and ticks in that swamp will eat you up.

One day when we quit for lunch, I was so tired till I couldn't hardly stand up. The boss man told me, "Uncle Ed, don't set down here. Take your lunch and eat it at the well. Carry a jug and bring the rest of us back some water."

The well was about a mile and a half away. The others was restin. I went on to the well, finish the day's work, and never went back.

The boss told another guy workin there to tell me not to ask for a job again, 'cause he wasn't goin to give me one since I had quit him.

"He can wait till I ask him for one," I say.

BACK ON SHARES

Finally I got back on shares with Mr. Addison. "We got shut of you on account of the tractor." he told me. "And I think we got rid of the wrong man."

Other people had got to poisonin with BHC once every eight days. Mr. Addison didn't like BHC. He want to mix arsenic with molasses and mop it on the leaves, all over the cotton. If hands don't really want to, they ain't goin to do the job the way the boss wants. By the barrel he had that stuff mixed. Some of the hands would use it, and some of them wouldn't. It was a tedious job, and none of them thought it did much good.

This aggravate Mr. Addison. He call us together. "The boll weevil ain't just after the white man. He's after you colored too. Now I could have you usin BHC. But if I do that, it will burn you in the nose and in the throat, and some of you it will make plumb sick.

"I ain't thinkin just of myself. I don't ever come out here huntin and fishin on my land. But you do. And BHC poison the land and unfits it for anythin but cotton. After you use BHC, you can't plant sweet potatoes or any other root crops behind cotton. The wind blow that stuff everywhere. It ruin the land for your vegetable gardens.

"The birds will eat the insects that got BHC, and they'll die. Come a big rain and the water will run off the fields into the fishponds and kill the fish.

"People have different ways to dodge the boll weevils. This is the way I want to do it. I want you to help me."

After that some of them did a little better, but not much.

That year I was the only hand Mr. Addison had to come out of debt and make money. I did it by usin my idea as to what to do and not the idea of Mr. Huey Lindley, the new overseer, who claim the only way to make a crop was to go ahead and plow, wet or dry. The cotton come up good, but in June it rain almost every day and kept the ground boggy wet.

The other hands was workin for wages. Mr. Lindley had them sloshin around in the wet. He come to me. "Go ahead. The others are plowin."

I knowed not to work in the mud, 'cause if you do, your land will get hard and clodded and your crop won't grow. So I went rabbit huntin and fishin, waitin for my farm to dry off. Whenever I seed Mr. Lindley peepin around my place, I'd get me somethin to do. Maybe I'd hoe a few bushes, or I'd take me my Dixie turnin plow and bar off some corn comin up in the Bermuda grass, or fool around with the plow like I was repairin it.

Mr. Lindley was in the habit of comin around about once a week. One time I was settin under a tree. "You still layin around the house?" The next time he brung a man with him. "Ed, if you ain't goin to work your crop, I got another man that will."

"I'll work it," I told him. I wait two more days; my crop good and dry. Then I get out early with a scrape and scooter and stayed late. I really got my crop cleaned out.

The best part was that on fifteen acres I made eleven bales of cotton behind one mule. I come clean out of debt and cleared one hundred and sixty dollars. Mr. Lindley didn't do so good. Sun and drought come and made the ground hard and scald the crop. Most of the men under Mr. Lindley that year made one or two bales of cotton. Three was the limit. And on Mr. Addison's hundred-acre farm Mr. Lindley made fifteen bales of cotton.

Mr. Addison turnt him off. "Ed, I'm proud to know you. If Mr. Lindley had done as good as you, I'd be a lot better off."

"Yes, sir," I say, "you really need a good overseer." Mr.

Lindley wasn't no count. I was a good farmer, and I knowed how to get other people to really put out. I would have made a better overseer than Mr. Addison ever had.

He called hisself a good man. And other people, colored and white, called Colonel Addison a good man. But bein white, he was handicapped to where he couldn't see the overseer in me.

I could really farm, and Mr. Addison knowed it. By rights I was due to make somethin. "Mr. Addison," I say, "I want to farm on standin rent." That's the deal a tenant makes to pay so much rent an acre for the use of the land. The owner don't get nothin else. But rentin can be tough too. If you have a family, they mouths never close except over food. Until you make the crop, you'll more than likely need furnish money. The boss will get his 10 per cent interest.

If you don't pay your rent, the landlord can level on you and take your stock up to what you owe him. He can sell anythin you got.

Several ways to farm have been figured out to be justice if the boss and the tenant both do right. There's sharecroppin, or rentin, or thirds, or fourths. But it's hard to find a boss or a tenant who really want to be fair to the other.

"Well, go to it, Ed," Mr. Addison tell me when I ask about standin rent.

Mr. Addison was a sure enough lawyer. I've heard it said that if he was on the other side, you was a goner. But he didn't know nothin about farmin. He let us pay him five dollars an acre rent on land we planted in cotton and three dollars an acre for land in corn and velvet beans. That was a little too cheap.

I made an extra good crop that year and bought me a Model T Ford for seventy-five dollars cash. Mr. Addison told me I had got the big end of the stick and that for the next crop we was goin to be on shares.

Me and my brother-in-law, Tom Sparrow, figure the real reason Mr. Addison change our standin rent deal back to shares was that we sold our cotton in Rochelle for the market price. When you rentin, you supposed to get the privilege to sell to anyone you want and to gin your cotton anywhere you can get the best deal.

But Mr. Addison didn't like it that way. He want to buy cotton from his renters under the market price and to sell it in Savannah, Georgia. That way he got his lick at it. "I was expectin you to bring cotton to me. You and Sparrow took it to Rochelle."

So my rentin come to an end after just one year. If I had had my rathers, I would have been on standin rent. But I couldn't complain. I was back on shares, and I did get half. Mr. Addison had a divided crib to put the corn in, my half on one side and his half on the other. All around me there were tenants that didn't fare as good as me. ☆

The Story of the Century CONTINUED FROM PAGE 29

lawyers who had signed on to assist the defense and the prosecution, respectively. The subject was the disclosure that Lindbergh, who attended the trial daily and sat only feet away from Hauptmann, was carrying a handgun in a shoulder holster under his jacket (because of constant crank threats on his life). The following dialogue then ensued:

DEFENSE LAWYER: Say, aren't you worried Lindbergh will pull that gun out some day and plug Hauptmann right between the eyes?

PROSECUTION LAWYER: Now why would Colonel Lindbergh want to do anything like that?

DEFENSE LAWYER: I'm damned if I wouldn't.

Nonetheless in the attempt to answer the prosecution's powerful case Reilly, the chief defense counsel, employed a habitual tactic of his in murder trials. He tried to shift guilt for the crime onto an amalgam of dead persons and prosecution witnesses, in this case creating an unlikely cabal of Isidor Fisch, Hauptmann's acquaintance (dead); Oliver Whately, the Lindbergh butler (dead); Violet Sharpe, a housemaid for Mrs. Lindbergh's mother (dead); Betty Gow, the Lindbergh nursemaid, a prosecution witness; and "Jafsie" Condon, the star prosecution witness.

As for Hauptmann's possession of a hoard of ransom money, Reilly alleged that Fisch had left it with Hauptmann for safekeeping before returning to Germany to die in 1934, and that Hauptmann had helped himself to a portion of the funds in repayment of a debt owed him by Fisch. A brother and sister of Fisch came from Germany to the trial to rebut every aspect of Hauptmann's story.

In the final analysis, in any event, Hauptmann was no ordinary hardworking family man plucked from nowhere to serve as a scapegoat. A World War I machine gunner at seventeen, he was unable to get work in the early Weimar period and turned to crime. He did a prison term for mugging two young women on the street and burglarizing, among others, a burgomaster's house. Released on probation after four years in prison, he was soon rearrested for a series of factory burglaries but escaped jail and, with extraordinary determination, suffered hunger and extreme discomfort to stow away three times on German ships before finally making it to the United States in 1923—and to his death in the electric chair thirteen years later.

Since 1939, when he left newspaper work, David Davidson has been a novelist and a free-lance writer of television plays and documentaries.

Mallet, Chisel, and Curls

CONTINUED FROM PAGE 47

suppress and control the eleven states of the Confederacy rather than reclaim them.

Lincoln's successor, Vice President Andrew Johnson of Tennessee, was a man of principle, dedicated to carrying out Lincoln's policy of "malice toward none... charity for all." But Johnson proved himself woefully inept and uncompromising in his relations with Congress. The elections of 1866 gave Republicans solid majorities in each house, and they proceeded to override his frequent legislative vetoes and to implement their own harsh version of Reconstruction. They also contrived to impeach Johnson—and Vinnie Ream was to play a surprising role in this famous event.

The radical wing of the Republican Party, brilliantly but fanatically led by Thaddeus Stevens—described by one writer as having the emaciated appearance of "a white old rock drying in the sun"—plotted the impeachment strategy. Early in 1867 Congress enacted over Johnson's veto the Tenure-of-Office Act. The measure prevented the President from dismissing without Senate approval any new official whose appointment required confirmation by that body.

Convinced that the act was clearly unconstitutional, the President put it to a test by summarily firing Secretary of War Edwin M. Stanton and appointing General Grant in his place. Stanton barricaded himself in his office at the War Department while the wrath of Republican opinion came down on the President like a storm.

The radicals on Capitol Hill, armed at last with the kind of issue they had been waiting for, lost no time in exploiting it. A resolution of impeachment was swiftly drawn up and, on February 24, 1868, was passed overwhelmingly by the House. One week later eleven separate charges—some of them ludicrous—were drawn up to support the resolution. It appeared probable that, for the first time in the nation's history, a Chief Executive would be forced out of office before his term had expired.

The House appointed seven "managers of the impeachment," including the old and ailing Stevens as chief strategist and headed by General Benjamin F. Butler (the "butcher of New Orleans," as he was unfondly known in the South), a congressman from Massachusetts, as chief prosecutor. Attention now turned to the more moderate Senate, where the issue would be decided.

Although the leading impeachers at the outset wrote off as lost the twelve Senate Democrats, they knew they could still convict the President by the necessary two-thirds vote if they could keep all but six Republicans in the radical fold. To their dismay, however, a preliminary party caucus revealed

Grim Thaddeus Stevens was one of Vinnie's first subjects and remained her friend.

that precisely six courageous Republicans believed that the evidence introduced to support the eleven Articles of Impeachment was not sufficient to convict the President. A seventh Republican, Senator Ross, refused to divulge his intentions. Although the radicals were shaken by the Kansas freshman's reluctance, they still believed that Ross, who represented perhaps the most anti-Johnson state in the Union, would vote for conviction. And they were prepared to take any steps necessary to make certain he did.

Vinnie Ream was well along toward completion of the clay model of Lincoln when Ross became the storm center of the impeachment. Given the unrelenting pressures applied to the senator, and Vinnie's supposed influence on Ross, who still boarded with the Ream family, it was inevitable that she would be pulled into the vortex.

On the eve of the Senate vote of May 16 the radicals dispatched to the Ream home on North B Street Daniel Sickles, another tough ex-general, who had been military governor of the Carolinas until President Johnson had recalled him for being too arduous in the execution of his duties. When Vinnie answered the door, as Sickles later recalled, "I pushed my way in." The general got right to the point: "You know what I came here for. I came to save Ross. You can help me." Sickles proceeded to rehash the President's alleged crimes in an attempt to convince Vinnie that Ross's political salvation was in her hands. Vinnie had become inured to such approaches, however, and scarcely replied. Although she protested truthfully that Ross was staying elsewhere that evening, Sickles planted himself in a parlor chair and stubbornly waited in vain for him throughout the night, with a nervous and tired Vinnie his reluctant hostess.

Ross had suffered his own relentless harassment. On the same evening as the Sickles visit he received this telegram from home: "Kansas has heard the evidence and demands the conviction of the President." It was signed "D. R. Anthony, and 1,000 Others." The next morning, before going to the Senate chamber to vote, Ross replied:

To D. R. Anthony and 1,000 Others: I do not recognize your right to demand that I shall vote either for or against conviction. I have taken an oath to do impartial justice according to the Constitution and laws, and I trust that I shall have the courage and honesty to vote according to the dictates of my judgment and for the highest good of my country.

That day Ross and six other Republican senators saved Andrew Johnson by a single vote. Following the outcome the seven senators were pariahs in Washington and in their native states. "D. R. Anthony and Others" wired Ross that "Kansas repudiates you as she does all perjurers and skunks."

Vinnie's punishment likewise was swift in coming. Twelve days after the key Senate vote the House passed a resolution ordering her to vacate her studio. The pretext was that the room was needed as a prison for one Charles Woolley, who was believed to have been bribing senators to vote for acquittal and who had refused to answer some of Butler's questions during a freewheeling radical investigation following the Senate decision.

Vinnie, however, proved to be considerably more popular than her unfortunate friend Senator Ross. Much of the nation's press was outraged at the House's peremptory action, and some editors flew into alliterative paroxysms. The *New York Times* of May 30 saw the move as a "paltry piece of petty persecution," while Washington's *Daily National Intelligencer* branded it a "wretched piece of petty malevolence and partisan proscription."

The New York *World*, however, topped even that. In a front-page article headlined "How Beaten Impeachers Make War on Women," the *World* said that if Butler ("this creature too flatteringly called 'the Beast'") and his colleagues were to have their way, there would be nothing left of the clay model of Lincoln "save a shattered, shapeless mass, to be moistened after it is too late, by a young girl's tears."

Not all of the press was on the sculptor's side, however. The New York *Tribune*, a persistent critic, attacked the "kitten-hearted Washington correspondents" who had leaped to Vinnie's defense:

This young woman, who is spoken of as "a helpless girl," had shown herself abundantly able to look out for her own interest, by the most persistent, unwearied, and successful lobbying in Washington for a whole Winter for the purpose of procuring this commission. She lobbied as only a woman can; and every Senator and Representative in Washington knows, by fearful experience, the terrible force of what has come to be known as "hen power."

Vinnie was even accused of passing off her former mentor's work as her own. But a letter found in her personal papers and signed by Clark Mills reads:

Whereas it has been reported that Miss Vinnie Ream is using a head of Mr. Lincoln modeled by me, on the statue she is making of Mr. Lincoln and whereas the statement is a base falsehood started doubtlessly for the purpose of injuring her. I herewith declare that it is her own work and modeled by herself in clay, and I deny the statements that I have reported otherwise.

Although Vinnie was required to remove her other works of art from the studio, she prevailed upon the sergeant at arms to allow her to leave the Lincoln model in place. To remove it in its clay state, she pled, would be to destroy long months of labor. Then, desperate to salvage her precious statue, she turned to the one friend who might have the power to help her: Thaddeus Stevens. Dying, and bitterly disappointed over the failure to remove President Johnson from office, Stevens nonetheless interceded on Vinnie's behalf. On July 20, less than two months after it had ordered her out of the Capitol, the House passed another resolution, permitting her to use the room for another year.

"Congress has again disposed of the weighty case of Miss Vinnie Ream," commented the *New York Times*. ". . . Justice and mercy are equally beautiful." Vinnie sent Stevens some flowers and wrote him a warm note the day after the resolution that said, in part: "But for you this result so important to me, could not have been. . . . May your life, so full of usefulness to your country and humanity be full of happiness—This is the earnest prayer of your faithful little friend. Vinnie Ream."

Early the following year Vinnie completed the plaster model of the statue and exhibited it in her studio to members of Congress. A leading American art expert, Miner Kilbourne Kellogg, also viewed the model. "The proportions of the figure are very exact," he reported, "an extraordinary merit which well repays the years of silent and laborious study given by Miss Ream to modelling the entire anatomy of the figure before casting the drapery upon it. . . . I shall wait with no little impatience to view this statue in pure and translucent marble. . . ." An enthusiastic Congress, no doubt relieved at this vindication of its confidence in Vinnie, paid her five thousand dollars as specified in the contract.

With the money secured, and with two pet doves and her parents in tow, the indomitable Vinnie set sail for Europe, the carefully wrapped plaster model resting in the hull of the ship. Pursuing her art in Paris and Rome,

One of Vinnie's most charming works was her impression of the Greek poet Sappho.
BOTH: LIBRARY OF CONGRESS

she also toured some of the Continent's famous art museums. Everywhere she went, Vinnie proved as popular in Europe as she had been in Washington.

She established a studio in Rome and selected a flawless slab of white Carrara marble for the Lincoln statue. After six months of arduous work the statue was finished, and Vinnie returned to the United States. Her moment of truth came shortly thereafter —in January of 1871, when members of Congress and other government officials, journalists, and personal friends gathered in the Rotunda to view the statue prior to its public unveiling. An Illinois delegation comprising individuals who had known the living Lincoln intimately were in the audience as the veil was slowly raised.

"There was a momentary hush, and than an involuntary, warm, and universal demonstration of applause gave the verdict of the distinguished and critical gathering, and assured the artist that her work was to be set down a success," commented *The Evening Star* of Washington. "... And then everybody turned to where the little sculptor-girl stood, a little in the rear with glad tears in her eyes, and congratulations were poured in upon her...."

At the lavish public unveiling later that month Senator Matthew Carpenter of Wisconsin said that "if she has failed at all, it is in presenting a statue more attractive than the original. But failing in this is no impeachment of her genius, for God only could make a face so sad, so rugged, so homely as Lincoln's was." Senator Lyman Trumbull of Illinois added that "it was fit that he who, by his own unaided efforts, had risen from obscurity to the highest earthly position, and who had gone down to the grave mourned by the civilized world, should have his features transmitted to posterity by one who, like him, had nothing but her hands and her head to urge her forward."

Vinnie's achievement brought her both fame and new opportunity. At the age of thirty-one she interrupted her work to marry Lieutenant Richard L. Hoxie of the United States Army Engineers in a ceremony considered brilliant even by Washington standards. She then completed a heroic statue of David Glasgow Farragut, famed Civil War admiral, which had been commissioned by Congress. The statue was cast in bronze from the propeller of Farragut's flagship, the U.S.S. *Hartford*, and placed in Farragut Square in the heart of the city. Although Vinnie, who became a popular Washington hostess, would later do other works as well, including two for Statuary Hall in the Capitol, she would be best remembered as the girl who sculptured Lincoln.

A century later millions of visitors to the Capitol each year pause before the statue of Abraham Lincoln, struck by its aura of simplicity and sadness. Few, however, know that the statue, one of the nation's great art treasures, was executed by a young girl. Nor do they know how close a vindictive Congress came to reducing the statue merely to Vinnie Ream's fond dream.

When Vinnie Ream was commissioned to do the official statue of Abraham Lincoln in 1866, Congress—somewhat carried away by her girlish charm—threw in a Capitol studio free.
CULVER

Stephen W. Stathis is an analyst in American history on the staff of the Library of Congress; Lee Roderick is Washington correspondent for a chain of newspapers located primarily in the western states.

The Don Quixote of Opera
CONTINUED FROM PAGE 56

ever. And little was heard from Max after that. In 1883, the year the Metropolitan Opera House opened, he did come out of retirement to conduct four operas—*Faust, Der Freischütz, Martha,* and *La Traviata*—at the Lexington Avenue Opera House. On opening night at the Met, Max was in the audience. He ran across Henry Abbey, the general manager, and said: "You'll lose $300,000 this season." Actually the Metropolitan Opera lost $275,000. The music critic Henry Krehbiel once encountered Max standing forlornly outside the new opera house. "Well," he told Krehbiel, "when I heard the house was to be built, I did think—I did think that some of the stockholders would remember what I had done for opera. . . . I thought somebody might remember this and the old man, and come to me and say, 'Max, you did a great deal for us once, let us do something for you now.' I didn't expect them to come and offer me the house, but I thought they might say this and add: 'Come, we'll make you head usher,' or 'You can have the bar.' But nobody came, and I'm out of it completely."

Yet he was not altogether forgotten, and on February 12, 1889, friends and admirers took over the Metropolitan Opera for a concert honoring the fiftieth anniversary of the old man's debut as an opera conductor in the United States. Such important conductors as Theodore Thomas, Anton Seidl, Frank van der Stucken, Adolph Neuendorff, and Walter Damrosch contributed their services. Eminent musicians sang and played. Max must have been pleased. He made a speech. The presence of such a large audience, he said, repaid him for the trials, the troubles, and all of the vicissitudes of fifty years. He said he had been asked many times how he had managed to keep opera going for thirty years, while others who had more brains and money than he had, had given it up in three or four years. The answer, Max said, was simple; it was because they had more brains than he had.

That was Max's last public appearance. Eight years later, on May 14, 1897, while living in obscurity in Pleasant Plains, Staten Island, he had a heart attack and died at the age of seventy-six.

Senior music critic of the New York Times, *Mr. Schonberg is a Pulitzer Prize winner and the author of many books on the history of music.*

Men of the Revolution
CONTINUED FROM PAGE 35

troops at the precise level of their capabilities. In January of 1781 Morgan was retreating before Banastre Tarleton's legion and decided to make a stand at a place called "the cowpens," where cattle were often wintered. It was not a choice many officers would have made. The site was a hilly meadow; beyond was the Broad River, cutting off any possible retreat in that direction; and by taking position on the hill Morgan was exposing his flanks, inviting a superior enemy to surround and annihilate him. But he had in mind a particular disposition of his troops, and the battleground suited him perfectly. In the front ranks he placed his militia—notorious for running away from battle; and before the engagement he told them that all he wanted was two rounds, two well-placed shots from each man, after which they could withdraw to the rear. One hundred and fifty yards behind this line was another, and these militiamen got similar instructions: hold your fire until the British come into close range, pick out the officers, and fire; then retreat to the third line when the enemy gets too close for comfort. In the rear was his main battle line, and here he posted his veterans—Delaware and Maryland Continentals and two hundred Virginia riflemen—and behind them a reserve. Finally, off to the left were William Washington's cavalrymen, with orders to swoop in on Tarleton's right flank when the moment was ripe.

The night before the battle Morgan made the rounds of his troops, bucking them up with praise, telling them exactly what he wanted of them. He saw to it that they were well fed and rested, and at dawn, when Tarleton launched his attack, Morgan's plan went off to perfection, almost totally destroying the larger, more experienced British force, costing the enemy over three hundred casualties (including sixty-six officers) and six hundred prisoners out of the eleven hundred troops engaged, against twelve Americans killed and sixty wounded. In saving his own little army to fight again Morgan also deprived Lord Cornwallis of an essential part of his—the light troops he needed most in the months to come. More important, perhaps, the battle raised the morale of rebels everywhere at a dark hour, encouraging southern militiamen to turn out in substantial numbers.

After Cowpens, Morgan's fighting days were at an end. Sciatica compelled him to return to Virginia, where he came so close to dying, he said, that he "literally peeped . . . into the other world." But he was not done for yet. After the war he operated a gristmill, speculated in western lands, corresponded regularly with his "old swords," took the field briefly during the Whiskey Rebellion as commander of a Virginia militia outfit, and in 1797 won a seat in the House of Representatives. In 1802 the Old Wagoner grudgingly gave up the fight and returned—doubtless struggling every step of the way—to his Maker. ☆

Johns Hopkins CONTINUED FROM PAGE 33

York, including Roosevelt, Bellevue, New York, and Presbyterian, he was a tireless and driven worker who managed somehow, in his spare time, to run a sort of tutoring course for those medical students who wished to pay for it. Dr. Arthur Stout, an associate of Halsted's during those days, recalled later that a medical student "got his real training from two sources, his preceptor and the private quiz. Every student had to be registered with a preceptor who must be a regular physician or surgeon—this practically amounted to an apprentice system . . .—and the young graduate's future might be assured if his preceptor was a person of influence." The private quiz, Halsted's favorite teaching device, "took the place of the conferences and quizzes which exist today in the Medical School itself. From three to six doctors would associate themselves under the leadership of the most prominent member and invite the medical students to recite to them by heart the various subjects which they studied [in lecture]." This was a valuable asset to any student who could afford the hundred-dollar fee, as he would be taken around to laboratories, dispensaries, and hospitals to witness practical demonstrations. The inexhaustible Halsted was also a popular host at his town house on East Twenty-fifth Street, where with his roommate, a fellow doctor, he gave dinner parties at least once a week, often with musical entertainment. Friends were welcome at a perpetual open house.

As a surgeon Halsted was incomparable. He was constantly searching out new operating techniques and partially incorporated the antiseptic theories of Joseph Lister. He became fascinated with solving the problem of trauma to the tissues during surgery, exercising great care to control bleeding and avoid cutting or tearing tissues wherever possible. Then, in 1884, he got word from Germany of a revolutionary new practice that was to change his life: he learned to inject cocaine, the first local anesthetic of its kind, into the cornea of the eye. Using himself as a guinea pig, he soon discovered that the drug enabled him to go for days on end without sleep and still feel clear-headed and exhilarated. He did not know until it was too late that he had become totally addicted. The exhilaration wore off, and Halsted became so debilitated that he could hardly function at all. Devastated, he entered the Butler Hospital for mental disorders in Providence in 1885, a human wreck.

Welch, saddened at this news of his former colleague, was determined to help him back to his feet. He went to Providence in December of 1886 and asked Halsted to come to live and work with him in Baltimore, offering him a job as a researcher in the pathology laboratory. For the next few years Halsted concentrated on his experiments, finally overcoming his dependence on cocaine. He would not touch a human patient during this time—he operated only on dogs but is said to have treated them as carefully as he would a man or woman. He discovered the benefits of silk as a suture and ligature, far better than the bulkier catgut (and still used); he experimented constantly with all sorts of new and improved clamps, scalpels, needles, and other surgical instruments.

Although eventually he resumed operating on humans, he was no longer William Halsted, the dynamic, self-confident New York surgeon. During his fight against cocaine his personality had undergone such a radical alteration that he bore only a ghostly resemblance to his former self. Once ebullient, lightning-fast, and indefatigable, he was now quiet, deliberate, and introspective. According to Donald Fleming, one of William Welch's biographers, "a 'Halsted' became a synonym for an operation drawn out to interminable length. . . . 'Would you mind moving a little?' he said to one of his assistants after a long operation. 'You've been standing on my foot for the last half hour.'" As Welch himself wrote much later about this dramatic change in Halsted, "While brilliancy, boldness and manual dexterity were attributes which I used to hear applied to Halsted as a surgeon in New York, these were precisely the qualities which in Baltimore he resented and desired to be substituted by conscientiousness, thoroughness and safety."

Now Welch had his head of surgery. The next step was to find the most capable clinician in the country, if not the world.

William Osler was a Canadian-born physician who had already established an admirable record in his field by the time Welch went after him. Although attracted to theology as a youth, he abandoned this interest and switched to medical school at the age of nineteen, graduating from McGill in 1872. He rose swiftly in his new profession: studies in Europe were followed by a professorship at McGill Medical School, a fellowship in the Royal College of Physicians in London, and, finally, an appointment as professor of clinical medicine at the University of Pennsylvania. An outgoing, humorous, and extremely popular man, Osler was always playing pranks on his fellows—when he was sixteen, he and a friend answered an advertisement in the local Toronto paper put in by a hapless American looking for a wife; they dressed up in women's clothes and met him at the station. But Osler was considered the best in his field and much sought after by hospitals all over the country. At a convention of the Association of American Physicians in Washington, D.C., in September, 1888, Billings, the hospital front man, began to court the illustrious Osler diligently, pressing him to take charge of the new medical department at Hopkins. Osler apparently was impressed, for he gave his consent to become the first physician-in-chief shortly thereafter. Welch was delighted; he wrote to his sister, saying: "[Osler] is the best man to be found in the country and it is a great acquisition for us to secure him. I know him well and have the highest opinion of him as a scientist and as a man."

The fourth and final member of that famous "first faculty" of Hopkins, appointed in 1889, was Howard A. Kelly, an obstetrician-gynecologist from Philadelphia and a protégé of Osler's. The only one of the four to be both American-born and American-trained, Kelly was a graduate of the University of Pennsylvania Medical School in 1882 and thereafter its professor of obstetrics. Among his few quirks was a lifelong fascination with snakes. He was adept in the operating room but not possessed of the brilliance of his three new colleagues. Nicknamed the "Kensington colt" because of his dedication to treating the poor of that Philadelphia suburb, he was a staunch conservative who, according to one of Welch's biographers, "always conducted a prayer-meeting for nurses, surgeons, and observers before operating."

The nucleus of the new hospital and medical school was now complete. There was considerable resentment among the local medical men that none of them had been chosen to head a department, not to mention the threat of all those outsiders taking away their business. But Welch quashed their fears. First, in 1885 he hired as his assistant pathologist a well-known Baltimorean, Dr. William T. Councilman; then he initiated a policy whereby all professors of preclinical subjects were to be in the full-time employ of the medical school so that they would devote all their time to teaching and research and have none left over for practice. This was considered a revolutionary step in medical education.

The construction of the hospital, as has been noted, took twelve years. Billings' plan, which aroused much interest both at home and abroad for its progressiveness, called for each ward to have an open area at the southern end, permitting the entry of lots of light and air. There would be two-story wards, each level connected by outside stairways. Billings intentionally omitted elevators in hopes of preventing "contaminated air" from passing between levels. Only the latest in heating and ventilation systems were to be installed. Those buildings to house patients with contagious diseases were to have separate cubicles for each individual, each cubicle to open onto a well-ventilated corridor that would permit breezes to blow through. Typical and impressive are these construction statistics for the year 1887: 8,200 lights, 1,200 kegs of nails, 44 miles of pipe, and more than a half mile of wrought-iron railing. When the hospital officially opened on May 7, 1889, there were seventeen buildings, among them four ward buildings, one isolation building, two private-patient buildings, a pharmacy, a nurses' dormitory, a kitchen, a bathhouse, and an administration building. There were some two hundred beds, just over half what Johns Hopkins had called for. The public came to gape and stare, to amble through the corridors and examine the wards. Eight days later the first patient was admitted.

The staff organization was also unusual. Each service (i.e., surgical, medical, pathological, obstetrical) was to be supervised by one man, who would have sole responsibility for what happened on that service. He would also, upon the opening of the medical school, be responsible for the teaching of his specialty. Osler's radical proposal was that each department head have under him a resident assistant, that is, a medical-school graduate who had completed his internship and would have complete authority when his chief was not about. The system proved invaluable, filling the gaping hole between inexperienced intern and busy professor (or, as it is now, practicing physician), and has been in general use ever since.

And the hospital was doing business. During that first year there were so many visitors to the dispensary (up to two hundred a day) that a charge of ten cents a patient was instituted—for those who could pay. Unfortunately there were no sinks equipped with running water in the wards, so after an operation the doctor had to scrub in a portable wooden washstand filled by pitchers, and when he couldn't get an orderly to empty it right away, the dirty water often overflowed onto the floor.

Meanwhile the hospital staff began to get impatient for the medical school to open. After all, the university had been open since 1876, and those undergraduates studying this new course called premed were being turned away to rival medical schools.

The problem, a very common one, was financial. It seemed that Johns Hopkins had left his country retreat and all his Baltimore & Ohio stock to the university, and all his bank stock and the remaining real estate to the hospital. The country retreat had had to be sold to the city as a park; and a terrible situation had arisen with the B&O stock: it had plunged disastrously in value, to the point where no dividend was paid between 1888 and 1891. The trustees could not invade the principal and began to worry lest Harvard and the University of Pennsylvania succeed in wooing Osler and Welch away before the medical school even opened. The situation was complicated by the fact that since the medical school was technically and legally a part of the university and not the hospital, none of the latter's funds could be used for it.

Into this bleak and unhappy dilemma stepped Martha Carey Thomas, a trustee's daughter and an English professor at Bryn Mawr College, and her friend Mary Garrett, daughter of the head of the B&O, who saw a way to advance the cause of women in medicine. They offered to form a national Women's Fund for the Higher Medi-

Martha Carey Thomas

cal Education of Women to raise money for the school—on condition that the admission requirements for women be the same as for men. The trustees, knowing they were in a tight corner, grudgingly agreed, but only if the ladies could raise the seemingly impossible sum of $500,000.

Welch, the newly appointed dean, and President Gilman were against it from the start. Welch indicated much later that his hesitancy sprang from a distaste at having to explain "indelicate things" to ladies. Although Osler, Kelly, and others were anxious to get the agreement settled and sent in a supporting letter, Welch's signature was conspicuously absent.

By 1892 the faculty of the nonexistent school was growing restive. Osler was sorely tempted to return to McGill, which was dangling a $1,000,000 chair before his nose; and Harvard was still after Welch. The Women's Fund was nowhere near its goal, having raised less than $200,000. But Miss Garrett, an early feminist and a woman of considerable personal wealth, was not to be thwarted. She would put up the remaining $306,977 but now tacked on even more stringent demands: not only were women to be admitted on an equal footing, but all candidates would have to have an A.B. degree or its equivalent, a reading proficiency in French and German, and knowledge of chemistry and biology as well as Latin, mathematics, and physics. And there was to be a four-, instead of a three-, year curriculum. These were by far the toughest admission standards ever contemplated for any medical school in the country. Osler, on hearing the latest proposal, commented to Welch: "We are lucky to get in as professors, for I am sure that neither you nor I could ever get in as students."

The administrators of Hopkins had, they said, eventually planned to gradually introduce more rigid standards for admission, but certainly not before the school even got off the ground. In fact, Welch later recalled that he had set down these idealistic terms years before in a letter to Gilman not long after arriving in Baltimore. He surmised that Miss Garrett had gotten hold of the letter through her lawyer, a member of the board of trustees. But, he declared, "It is one thing to build an educational castle in the air at your library table, and another to face its actual appearance under the existing circumstances."

The trustees knew that they were trapped. First they tentatively agreed but haggled over Miss Garrett's stipulation that women be admitted "on the same terms" as men. Why not just substitute "equivalent" or "equal" for the word "same"? they asked. Miss Garrett stubbornly refused and in exasperation made it a further condition that all the funds revert back to her or her estate should there be a violation of her wishes. On December 24, 1892, the trustees finally gave in.

To prepare the best possible curriculum President Gilman sent out a questionnaire, describing the proposed courses, to various medical scholars in both the United States and Great Britain. To his delight the response was highly complimentary. But then everyone began to worry about how they would ever get enough qualified applicants to make the whole project worthwhile. They needn't have. By the time this new branch of the university opened in October, 1893, eighteen students had enrolled —fifteen men and three women—although they *were* outnumbered by their teachers. Five were graduates of Johns Hopkins University, having been well prepared by the new premedical course. There were even an additional forty-odd physicians doing graduate work. Among the courses studied that first year were osteology, histology, physiological chemistry, and, of course, anatomy. The anatomy professor, Franklin P. Mall, was inclined to let the students learn by trial and error rather than by lecture, so he would give each a knife and then leave the room. This at first was a bit frustrating for the students. He was just as eccentric when examination time came, as he disliked this sort of formality; so he would simply take each student for a walk in the park, and after discussing such totally irrelevant topics as Paris fashions, he would suddenly pull a fragment of bone out of his pocket and demand: "What is this?" Though they all guessed wrong—it was a turtle bone—he passed them.

Mall had a problem at first getting sufficient cadavers, so the dissection part of the anatomy course was postponed until November. When bodies became more plentiful, Mall had a large icebox built, embalmed the bodies with carbolic acid, and stuck them away. But a larger problem awaited him: when classes began, he spied across the dissecting room one day a lovely young woman named Mabel Glover, a Wellesley graduate and one of the three female students in the class. By spring they were engaged, leading Osler to comment wryly when speaking about Hopkins to the Harvard Medical Alumni Association that June: "When I tell you that $33\frac{1}{3}$% of the lady students admitted to the first year of the Medical Faculty of the Johns Hopkins University are, at the end of one short session, to be married, then you will understand why I saw that co-education is a failure. If we lose $33\frac{1}{3}$% at the end of the first session where will the class of lady students be at the end of the fourth?" (Some time later he was appalled to learn that another of those first lady students had dropped out after her conversion to Christian Science.)

Meanwhile hospital business went on as usual. While awaiting the arrival of the first medical-school graduates, the house staff positions were filled by graduates of other institutions. Under the supervision of the four chiefs (Halsted had been appointed associate professor of surgery in October, 1889, and then promoted to full professor in 1892) the students were allowed to come directly into the wards to observe those diseases about which they had been lectured. Once again this was an exciting innovation, earning Hopkins its reputation as the first teaching hospital in America. As the Flexners put it in their biography of Welch, at last "laboratories took the place of the lectures traditional in American medical schools—the hospital patient was nature's laboratory— and experiments the place of precepts. ... Almost immediately the young men and women began to taste the joys of self-training, because so much of their time was placed at their own disposal and they were so closely in contact with their professors."

Welch, Osler, and Halsted, because of their relative youth, were quickly adopted by the staff doctors as friends as well as teachers and dubbed "Popsy," "the Chief," and "the Professor," respectively. The genial Welch, as dean of the medical school, was caught up more in administration than in clinical work but did manage to keep up his lectures in pathology; he was enormously proud of Halsted and wrote to a friend: "The number of patients surpasses all anticipations and Halsted (popularly known in hospital circles as Jack the Ripper) does nothing but operate the whole forenoon and it must be admitted with brilliant results." Welch himself was making quite a name for Hopkins, for his reputation as an outstanding pathologist had spread to Europe. While attending an international conference in Berlin in 1890 he had been voted an honorary president of the pathological section, and now doctors from all over the East were coming to do research in Welch's laboratory, among them Major Walter Reed. A further accolade that demonstrated Baltimore's acceptance of Welch was his election in 1891 to the presidency of the Medical and Chirurgical Faculty of Maryland, the elite society of the state's physicians.

Welch's original faith in Halsted was more than justified. Now an aloof, reserved man, the "Professor" discouraged, by his formal, austere presence and caustic wit, most associates from becoming intimate, but as a surgeon he drew enormous attention at home and from abroad to his teaching and operative clinics. His greatest pleasure was training surgeons; and realizing that the best way to teach them was to show them, he would perform operations before their eyes on his old wooden operating table, left over from the Franco-Prussian War, with its deep trough and drainage hole. He was always inventing ways to ease the surgeon's task; when a nurse complained of a severe rash on her hands and arms after scrubbing in carbolic acid, he asked the Goodyear Rubber Company to make two pairs of rubber gloves for him, as thin as possible. No one had ever thought of such a thing.

Kelly and Mencken and God

Dr. Howard A. Kelly did not limit his religious fervor to prayer meetings held prior to surgery. In an article in the February 6, 1975, *New England Journal of Medicine*, Dr. Laurence E. Karp tells of Kelly's meddlesome attempts at "religious-oriented civic uplift" that led to a series of well-publicized squabbles with the formidable H. L. Mencken. Karp describes how, after sharing a train ride with Kelly from Washington to Baltimore one day, Mencken became so provoked that "three separate times I was on the point of jumping out of the train-window." It seems that Kelly, raised in a family of clergymen, made it his business to try to persuade others to share his fundamentalist views. He sometimes wore a lapel button embossed with a question mark and would query people he met as to its meaning—which he called "the most important question in life." After stumping his victim with this riddle he would jubilantly exclaim: "The most important question is, What think ye of Christ? Whose Son is He?" Kelly also had a habit of waiting until his taxi had pulled up to a red light, then preaching at the driver: "Cabby, I hope when you and I come to the gates of heaven, the light will be green."

Somehow Kelly found time between patients to serve as coeditor of the *Christian Citizen*, for which he wrote editorials advocating the Sunday closing of places of entertainment and, predictably, Prohibition. Mencken retaliated in the Baltimore *Evening Sun:* "[Kelly] happens to be a man I have long known, and in every respect save the theological, greatly respected. But in that theological aspect... he is so plainly a menace to the peace and dignity of this town that what he believes should be made known to everyone, that the people may be alert to his aberrations and keep a curb on his public influence. If he had his way... life here would be almost impossible to civilized men. He is against practically everything that such men esteem, at least in the way of relaxation and recreation, and he is moved by a perfect frenzy to put his prejudices into harsh and unintelligent laws."

Kelly paid little attention to his critic, who referred to him as "Dr. Evangelicus." He ran—unsuccessfully—for the Maryland Assembly in 1921, his platform based on "no liquor, no racetrack gambling, no unnecessary paid labor on Sunday." Mencken exulted that the voters had refused to be taken in by Kelly's "whole scheme of sanctification by force," adding: "How long are the people of Baltimore going to stand this nuisance?"

Yet, surprisingly, the two harbored no deeply embedded antagonism toward each other. Kelly referred to "dear Brother Mencken," vowing, "I am a friend of his and hope someday to win him." Mencken returned the compliment: "We do not estimate the integrity and ability of an acquaintance by his flabby willingness to accept our ideas; we estimate him by the honesty and effectiveness with which he maintains his own." On Kelly's seventy-fifth birthday Mencken wrote: "More than once [Kelly and I] have been on opposite sides of some public matter, but every contact with him... has only increased my admiration for his immense energy, his unbreakable resolution, and his complete honesty. Baltimore owes him a lot."
—*C.J.F.*

Perhaps it could be said that Halsted's greatest contribution to surgery was his pioneer work in the treatment of breast cancer. In the eighteenth century a French surgeon had made the connection between this form of cancer and lymphatic glands, but it was Halsted a century later who performed the first radical mastectomy. He was very successful with his surgery for hernias as well.

The one vestige of the precocaine Halsted was his expensive taste. His suits were made in London, his shoes —of which he ordered six pairs at a time—and shirts in Paris (the shirts were sent back by ship to be laundered at regular intervals), and he could often be spotted walking the hospital corridors in frock coat and tall silk hat. His love of elegance ruled the household after he married his head nurse, Caroline Hampton, in 1890; *he* selected the antiques and Persian rugs that filled their Baltimore town house and their summer cottage in the mountains of North Carolina, and when they entertained, *he* would select the china, food, linen, and flowers. Often he and Welch would dine together at the staid Maryland Club on terrapin and Chesapeake oysters.

Osler was probably the best liked of all. A small, slender man of dark complexion, he too dressed in frock coat and top hat. Consistently cheerful and outgoing, possessed of a lively sense of humor, he disliked gossip or criticism and was remarkably modest. He wrote prolifically of his clinical findings and was widely published in medical journals; once in a while he mischievously submitted articles under the unlikely nom de plume "Edgerton Y. Davis of Caughnawauga, P.Q." He brought his students into the wards and put them to work applying dressings and keeping charts; he called his hand-picked interns "A.A.I. copper-bottomed young graduates." He tried to instill in these students his own love of his work, based on untiring thoroughness and the ability to reason things out. His *Principles and Practice of Medicine*, published in 1891, became the definitive text of internal medicine and was eventually translated into Spanish, French, German, and Chinese.

Osler's particular bêtes noires were typhoid fever, pneumonia, and tuberculosis, and his researches led him to become an ardent public-health reformer. He cared nothing for the lucrative side of medicine and private practice, being much more concerned with bringing Johns Hopkins' desire to life: to open the hospital to the poor and the sick, regardless of their sex, age, or race.

By the early 1900's the hospital and medical school were solvent and universally respected, and some of those who had helped make them so could move on. Osler accepted an invitation to go to Oxford University, where he assumed the formidable title of Regius Professor of Medicine, and later that of baronet. Welch, although he remained in Baltimore the rest of his life, was satisfied that Hopkins was in a condition of relative stability and became involved with the Rockefeller Institute of Medical Research and the Carnegie Foundation as adviser and later a trustee. Intensely interested in medical and health conditions around the world, he travelled to such remote outposts as Peiping, China, and made such an impression there that he was later honored by the doctors of the Peiping Union Medical College on his eightieth birthday in 1930—and by President Hoover as well. The fact that Hopkins was never allowed to become a parochial, nonprogressive hospital is certainly due in large measure to Welch's unceasing desire to bring international advances in the field back to Baltimore.

Halsted remained at Hopkins the rest of his life, receiving almost as many honorary degrees as Welch and Osler. His contribution is best described by Professor René Leriche, an eminent French surgeon, who said in 1914: "Halsted has created a method in surgery and he has inspired disciples. It is this that gives his clinic such vivid originality, and when one has seen intimately that admirable organization one understands why Baltimore has rapidly become the cradle of contemporary surgery in the United States."

Construction continued into the 1930's, often funded by the great financiers of the time: the Rockefeller and Carnegie foundations; "Diamond Jim" Brady, a grateful patient who gave over $300,000; Henry Phipps, who gave money for the psychiatric clinic that still bears his name; James Buchanan's niece and hostess, Harriet Lane, who founded a pediatric clinic. When H. L. Mencken wrote a series of articles for the Baltimore *Sun* in 1937, he discovered that a phenomenal fifteen thousand patients were admitted annually; almost half of these paid nothing whatever, just as Hopkins had ordained. Today those figures have more than doubled, and the hospital can accommodate almost eleven hundred patients at one time. In 1974 there were just under a half million outpatient visits; and the rule, according to the public-relations director, is still "pay what you can." A new and major redevelopment program has rendered all but a few of the first plain red brick buildings into dust.

All this is a far cry from the days Welch described in a nostalgic letter to Howard Kelly in 1933, on the occasion of the latter's seventy-fifth birthday: "You will remember some of the mad pranks Osler used to play on your new patients. Osler, arriving early in the morning and learning that you had not seen [them yet], would say that he would prepare the patients for your visit by dropping in and informing [them] that [your] senile tremor disappeared as soon as you began to operate."

Perhaps Johns Hopkins would have been established as one of the finest hospitals and medical training centers in the world without these men; but it is doubtful. In any case, the name is still synonymous with medical expertise. A fine tribute to the institution made by Halsted's good friend Henry James when he came to Baltimore to see and admire in 1905 indicates the feeling Hopkins still inspires: "The great Hospital, with its endless chambers of woe . . . [has] turned . . . to fine poetry . . . the high beauty of applied science."

The author has close family ties with Hopkins. Her father is associate professor emeritus of orthopedic surgery there; her brother is an instructor and staff member.

POSTSCRIPTS TO HISTORY

EUTAW SPRINGS

Many readers rapped our knuckles for a serious gaffe we committed in the August, 1975, issue, where we said that the Battle of Eutaw Springs was fought in North Carolina. It took place, of course, in South Carolina. The most eloquent rebuke came from Sam P. Manning, who, as a South Carolina state representative, was chiefly responsible for having Cowpens—the site of Daniel Morgan's set-piece victory over "Butcher" Tarleton—named a national historic site. He is now working for similar recognition for Eutaw Springs. After correcting us on our mix-up about the state, Representative Manning went on to say that he thought our illustration, which showed the Americans drinking and looting toward the end of the fight, did them a grave disservice:

The picture is unfair to the brave men who fought and died at Eutaw Springs. It does not convey in any sense the valor, the courage, or the sacrifices of the men who fought in this battle, which was probably the hardest-fought of the Revolution. If General Greene had lost at Eutaw Springs, it is doubtful that General Washington would have risked victory or defeat at Yorktown. It is interesting to note that John Adams wrote that the significance of Eutaw Springs was of equal importance to Yorktown.

The Continental Congress awarded a gold medal to Greene in honor of Eutaw Springs. It was one of six gold medals struck in Paris under the supervision of Thomas Jefferson and Benjamin Franklin during 1785–6 to honor significant actions of the recent war. The largest medal was given to Washington for the retreat of the British from Boston; the second largest went to Greene for Eutaw Springs. The presentation of this medal to Greene is one of the eight scenes from history on the bronze doors of the United States House of Representatives.

At Eutaw Springs both the Continental soldiers and the militia served with great gallantry. Soldiers from at least eleven of the thirteen states fought in the battle. (Among them was Greene's orderly, a free black man from Maryland, who gave his life and was cited for bravery by Greene.) Over forty counties in twenty-one states are named in honor of the heroes of Eutaw Springs.

Your painting exaggerates in caricature one scene at the end of the battle but leaves out its meaning. Other paintings that AMERICAN HERITAGE has produced for other battles of less importance portray valor and patriotism; Eutaw Springs, one of the great battles of the war, deserves no less.

ANNA AND EMILIE

The turn-of-the-century picture below was just discovered and passed on to us by the New Jersey Historical Society. It shows Anna Lindner, whose water colors ran in the last issue. She is sitting in front of her Bayonne home with her niece, Emilie, whose early years Anna chronicled with painstaking devotion in scores of paintings.

MEDALLION: LOSSING, *Field Book of the Revolution*, 1860

LUSITANIA VICTIMS

In the introduction to Mrs. Theodate Pope Riddle's account of her rescue from the *Lusitania* (April, 1975) we said that nothing was known about Mme. Depage and Mrs. Naish. That this is not the case has been called to our attention by a dozen readers, among them Mrs. George D. Rowe of Baltimore, who writes:

I loaned a copy of this issue to a friend, Miss F. May Cooper, who went to England in June of 1915 with the American Red Cross and was transferred to a hospital at Lapanne, near Ostend, Belgium, the following year. She tells me that the head of that hospital was M. Depage and that his wife, Mme. Marie Depage, had been lost on the *Lusitania* while returning from a fund-raising campaign in America. Her body was washed ashore near Queenstown, Ireland. She remembers very well seeing the grave of Mme. Depage in a small plot near the hospital, overlooking the North Sea. It was enclosed by a low white picket fence and decorated with wreaths of flowers made of bright-colored beads.

Mrs. Naish suffered a happier fate, according to the Reverend Charles A. Platt of Ridgewood, New Jersey:

She was Mrs. Theodore Naish, who lived for many years after the tragedy in Kansas City. She was a close friend of my parents, and I recall vividly an evening she spent in our home (when I was nine) during which she told the story of the sinking and her rescue. She was on her honeymoon with her husband. When the first torpedo struck, she and her husband put on life jackets and went immediately to their assigned boat station. She recalled standing there holding her husband's hand, awaiting the launching of a lifeboat, when there was a second explosion, which sent her crashing into the deck above her head. The next thing she remembered was being pulled from the sea onto an overturned lifeboat. She never saw her husband again.

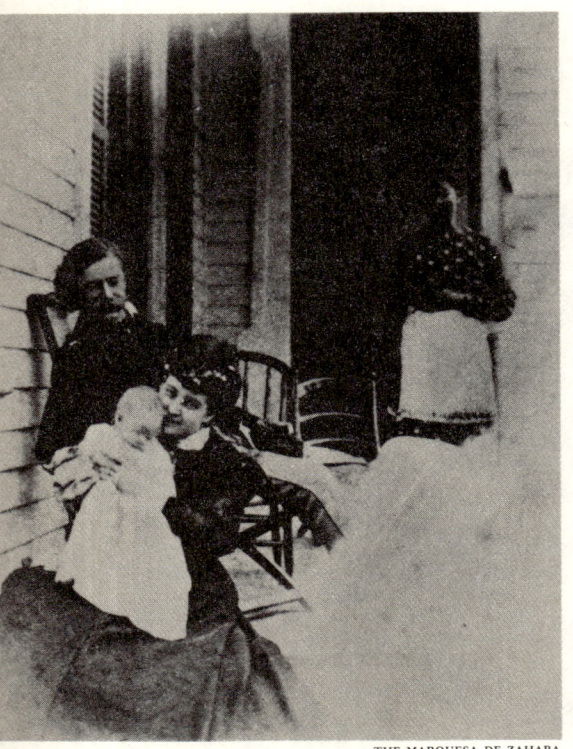

THE MARQUESA DE ZAHARA

THE PAST REVEALS ITSELF

In June of 1970, in an article entitled "The Past Springs Out of a Picture," we ran a photograph (above) identified as "General George Armstrong Custer ... with his wife, a maid, and their baby." We were quickly reminded by our readers that Custer never had a child. What, then, was the baby doing there?

Now, more than five years later, we are astonished to learn that the baby had every reason to be there, for the languid young officer was indeed its father.

Robert M. Utley, the western historian, has finally cleared up the mystery. "The fact is," writes Utley,

these people are not George and Elizabeth Custer but Albert and Jennie Barnitz. The black maid holds baby Bertha, who was born in this building (the officers' quarters at Fort Leavenworth) on March 26, 1870, and the Barnitzes left Fort Leavenworth for retirement on June 21, 1870, which establishes the time frame within which this picture was taken. I have a snapshot of these same four people on the same front porch; Barnitz indeed did resemble Custer, in his nose and his head full of curly blond hair. Note, too, that Barnitz wears the single row of buttons of a captain rather than the double row that Custer, as a lieutenant colonel, would have worn.

Barnitz was an energetic officer who served throughout the Civil War with the 2nd Ohio Cavalry. Afterward he obtained a Regular Army commission as captain of G Troop, 7th Cavalry, under his famous look-alike. He fought in the Cheyenne Indian wars of 1867–68 and was severely wounded at the Battle of the Washita. Invalided out of the service, he went on to lead a lively civilian life as a public speaker and traveller, and though he finally did die of his wounds, it was not until 1912. Robert Utley is currently editing his diaries and letters.